WHY DIDN'T ANYBODY TELL ME THIS SH*T BEFORE?

Wit and Wisdom from Women in Business

MARCELLA ALLISON
LAURA GALE

Titanides LLC

*To all the fearless, resilient, amazing women
we've met along the way, and to those we've yet to meet,
who inspire us with their stories and trust us with their truth.*

Thank you.

CONTENTS

WHY DIDN'T ANYBODY TELL ME THIS SH*T BEFORE?

Edited by Marcella Allison & Laura Gale

INTRODUCTION: MARCELLA ALLISON

All my life I've been one of the 'only women in the room'. I was a female entrepreneur in 1994 long before it was fashionable. I was one of only eight women in my MBA class. I was the only breast-feeding venture capitalist at my investment firm. I am one of a handful of top female financial copywriters. And I'm one of the few female CEOs in direct response advertising.

I've spent decades surrounded by smart, talented, successful, men. Lots and lots of men. And I've learned to adapt and survive and even thrive in all-male business settings.

But the truth is, it's the women who got me through it. It's the women I called when I was struggling to succeed. It's the women I confided in when I wasn't sure if I could hack it. It's the women who propped me back up when I wanted to quit. It's the quiet conversations with women in the hallways, in the ladies room, over glasses of wine in the bar that saved me.

Because it's the women who understand what it's like to be trapped in a business meeting and have breast milk leak all over your blouse. They know what it's like to have to pack your own suitcase, cook and freeze a weeks' worth of meals, and leave sixty pages of directions just to leave town for two days for a conference. They know how it feels to suffer through condescending 'mansplaining', inappropriate jokes, or endless sports metaphors without batting an eye.

Several years ago, I found myself at yet another conference without a single woman speaker on the stage. Not one. The conference was billed as 'the titans of the industry.' And every single presenter was a man.

When I realized this, I began searching the room for the women. Then I grabbed all the women I could find and I invited them to a small intimate dinner at the hotel that night. We ended up sitting around the table for hours, sharing the truth of our lives, both personal and professional. As the night ended, we decided that one night was not enough. We needed more.

So we formed our own private all-women's group and we called ourselves the Titanides. Because in Greek mythology, the Titanides are the six goddesses who rule heaven and earth (including the mother of the Muses). What better archetype for a group of female copywriters, marketers and entrepreneurs than a bunch of creative, bad-ass, take-no-prisoners, Greek goddesses who rule the world?

We decided to host our own conference for women only. We decided we were tired of waiting to be invited to speak. Instead, we decided to build our own stage.

At the first Titanides conference, I wanted to honor the spirit and tone of that first dinner. So I invited all of the speakers to write a letter to their younger selves imparting one piece of hard won wisdom. Then I asked the women to read their letters from the stage in between presentations.

When I sat down to read the reviews after the conference, I was shocked. While the attendees clearly appreciated and valued all the presentations, they were absolutely blown away by those letters. It was the raw honestly and vulnerability of smart talented women speaking publicly about the truth about their work and their lives that transformed that event into something life-changing.

That's when I finally understood that all those stories, all those private conversations in bathrooms and bars with other women, are vital to our survival in a male dominated world. That's when I knew that we had to make these letters public. And that's when the idea for this book was born.

Why Didn't Anybody Tell Me This Sh*t Before? is a book of collective mentoring for women, by women. Every woman in this book shares the truth of her life, her experience, and her past. Not because she wants fame or recognition. But because she wants to help another woman to succeed. Each of these women owns her truth, honors her experience, and shares her hard-won wisdom, whatever that might be.

Like the feminist poet Audre Lorde once wrote, I too "have come to believe over and over again that what is most important to me must be spoken, made verbal and shared, even at the risk of having it bruised or misunderstood."

Speaking as a black lesbian poet in a mostly white male world, she goes on to say, "I was going to die, if not sooner then later, whether or not I had ever spoken myself. My silences had not protected me. Your silence will not protect you."

While not all the women in this book would identify as feminist, the mere act of their speaking their truth and telling their stories is radical, risky, and transformational. That is why we call ourselves the "Not-So-Secret Order of the Titanides." Because the only way we can begin to change the world is if we break the silence and begin to speak.

In ancient Greece, Mnemosyne was the Titanide of memory and remembrance and the inventress of language and words. She was the mother of the Muses and the patron goddess of poetry and storytelling. And like our namesake, the Titanides in this book choose to remember.

We choose to tell the truth about what it means to be a wife, a daughter, a mother, *and* an entrepreneur or professional. We choose to talk about what it means to leave an abusive marriage, to lose your parents, to doubt yourself, and to fear failure and still keep going. We choose to talk about the choices we made, to own our successes and to learn from our mistakes.

It was Virginia Woolf who famously wrote, "A woman must have money and a room of her own if she is to write fiction." I would add that a woman needs money and a room of her own if she is to succeed in the business world as well.

The Titanides community (Titanides.com) is a room of our own, where women can share our truth with each other without having to explain, justify or defend ourselves... where our credentials are accepted without question... and where we can let down our guard without being judged.

It's a private place where we can share a glass of wine with each other and talk shop or shopping. Where we can discuss business or boyfriends, close deals or vent... all without worrying it will come back to bite us in the behind.

Most importantly, Titanides.com is a place where we inspire, empower, and mentor other women to succeed. Because all of us can benefit from being surrounded by more smart, talented, successful women.

Why Didn't Anybody Tell Me This Sh*t Before is our attempt to share this magical space with you. I hope you'll kick off your heels, grab a glass of wine and join us. I suspect that you will discover, as I did, that in reading these letters, you'll see your own story reflected back to you.

My wish is that you will find wisdom, strength, and hope from our past that will carry you into your even more brilliant future. And that collectively we will all create a better future for our daughters, our nieces, our goddaughters, our granddaughters and all the future female leaders of the world.

Marcella Allison, Founder of The Not-So-Secret Order of the Titanides

Cincinnati, 2019.

LETTER FROM THE EDITOR:
LAURA GALE

This book, more than any other project I've ever worked on, is a monument to honesty. So in the spirit of transparency you will find in these pages, let me begin with a confession.

I wanted to turn this book down.

For the last few years, my work has immersed me deep into the world of business—the world of data and metrics, where performance is everything and the personal is quarantined from the professional.

But Marcella fully embodies both the personal and professional in every moment. There is no distinguishing her formidable professional abilities from her buoyant, gleeful personal presence. She has an uncanny way of transforming difficult, jagged feelings into powerful, motivating material, and her enthusiasm to have me join the project gave me pause.

To borrow a line from Joyce—one of the contributors to this book—feelings have always been problematic for me, and there was no getting around the fact that this book was going to bring up a *lot* of feelings.

And that scared the ever-living shit out of me. Taking on a project where so many women would hand me their most challenging, vulnerable, triumphant moments felt like looking into a glacier ravine—so beautiful, and so very, very dangerous.

But someone far wiser than I once told me that every good thing is on the other side of fear.

I knew, from hard-earned experience, that the only way out is through, and that if I said no, I would be shutting out some vital piece of my future. So I said yes, and this book has been the most transformative experience of my working life.

Entrepreneurship, or an unconventional path in any part of life, can be immensely isolating. When I quit my job in publishing and struck out on my own, I could not find a single woman doing what I wanted to do, in the way I wanted to do it.

There were plenty of women in business, but I couldn't relate to any of them. They weren't *like* me, and I didn't want to be like them. I felt overwhelmed by how much that felt like orphanhood, and, per my difficulties in dealing with feelings, hoped that the panicked loneliness would just fade while I got on with building my business.

For the next few years I justified my intense resistance to seeking female mentorship with all manner of excuses. *She's in a different industry to me. She came up when the world was different. She's too feminist, she's trying too much to be one of the guys, she's too vanilla, she's too extreme.*

But when Marcella handed me the 20 original letters that inspired this project, I drew up sharp in front of all those justifications—and found them false. The Titanides were the women I had been missing all these years. (And you say that fun word tit-ah-nah-days.)

Those women, and the dozens of others who have joined this project since, have been through a gamut of incredible challenges. While many of them say they would never wish their experience on anyone, they're grateful and hopeful because of it —it taught them something about themselves. They found that they are tougher than they realized, more resourceful than they realized, and have stronger communities and networks around them than they realized.

Named for the descendants of the Greek Titans—the children of the primordial gods that emerged from the Cosmos before time began—the women from the Titanides community in this book are a profound reflection of those complex, beautiful, fierce women in the mythology.

The Greek goddesses and their descendents were a formidable group. They were warriors, leaders, creators, fiercely protective mothers, wives and patrons. They demanded their dues, and never allowed disrespect or dismissal to go unchecked. They believed themselves to be worthy of the best the universe had to offer. They knew what they wanted, and they used every tool at their disposal to get it.

Like us, they were not simple creatures, but complex, multifaceted characters. They could be generous and vengeful. Kind and manipulative. Creative and cruel. Mythology is powerful and timeless because we can relate so intensely to the stories and the characters that live them—they are *our* stories. We *are* them.

And yet, we are not them. The women in this community are not wrathful like the goddesses could be. They are not vengeful. They do not tear other women down to soothe themselves. Let me be clear that while none of the women in this book are perfect, they choose not to be ruled by their flaws.

The stories you will find in these pages are complex, and every woman's desire to come out better than she was has been all the more inspiring to me, because of that complexity. Many times their lessons are hard and painful, and there is no neat happy ending. These are not fairytales—they are battle stories.

Their lessons are hard-earned. The lessons have left scars. They have changed the structures of our lives. And there is a lot of comfort to be taken from that—we all live in a world that is increasingly complex, with ever more challenges to our autonomy and sense of self. In such an environment, you yourself can only be complex.

And whether we're on the entrepreneurial road or we're more 'intrapreneurial', we are all looking for insights into the personal and professional situations that take us to the edge of our abilities. This book is both lifeline and roadmap, and I encourage you to see that you are made from the same stuff as all these women.

Take courage, and borrow from their strength. Give yourself some grace, and learn from their lessons. And trust that the triumph, joy and hopefulness they have earned is waiting for you too.

If you see yourself reflected in these pages, I hope you'll join us in the Titanides community. You have a place with us, and we're waiting for you.

Laura Gale
Lisbon, 2019.

NOT-SO-SECRET
LESSON #1

LOVE YOURSELF FIRST AND EVERYTHING ELSE FALLS INTO LINE

≈

The famous American comedienne, Lucille Ball said, "Love yourself first and everything else falls into line. You really have to love yourself to get anything done in this world."

Lucille loved herself enough to get a lot done. She was the first woman to have creative control over her own television show. She co-owned the world's first independent television production company, Desilu Productions. And she became the first Hollywood female CEO when she bought her husband out.

For each of the Titanides in this chapter, loving yourself first is a conscious choice. For Jennifer, it means knowing her worth, taking a deep breath and asking for it. For Lori, it's six little words that remind her to put herself first and protect her boundaries. For Laura, it's the sudden realization that the savior she's been waiting for is herself, that the unbreakable woman inside is the one who will come to save her. For Billye, it's the sudden realization in a moment of crisis that she is built for bigger things, and the Universe has a plan for her. For Lorrie, it means looking inward for validation and realizing that self-love can only come from within, and for Lyn, it's the permission to simply be herself and to know that *that* is enough.

For many women, putting ourselves first is difficult. We tend to give more than we get. We let others take advantage of us, and we settle for scraps, until one day when we are finally forced to say that enough is enough.

Lucille Ball is such an amazing example here because she never settled for scraps. She was always fighting for herself and her dreams in a male-dominated world. Her famous TV character, Lucy, was always scheming and conniving to break into show biz. In real life, Lucy's company created some of the most enduring and profitable shows on television. And Lucille did it all because she loved herself, and believed that she was worthy and capable of doing great things.

So remember: if you want to get anything done in this world, you've got to love yourself first.

JENNIFER STEVENS

~

*Just because money isn't your first motivator, it doesn't mean you don't
deserve to get paid what you're worth.*

ON THE SLIPPERY RELATIONSHIP BETWEEN GIVING AND
Worth...

Dear Jen,

You tend to give more than you get. There's nothing wrong
with this in principle...

It's laudable to be helpful and thoughtful, to be conscientious
and generous, to just put your head down and do what needs
doing because somebody must.

There isn't a story of progress that doesn't include somebody
pushing on and getting the job done, never mind the
compensation or recognition. That's just not the point.

But when it comes to work, to your career... all that giving
isn't always in your own best interest. People know you'll get the
job done. So they let you do it.

And because you're one of those people who gets the job done... you tend to carry on, whether you're being properly compensated or not.

But you can't afford to function that way indefinitely. Not when it comes to earning an income and building a business. It undercuts your value. People start to say things like, "See if Jen will do it—she'll get the job done right. And she's cheap."

You can get the job done right and charge what you're worth. And you should. Because people will pay for it—when you ask them to. Part of the reason that women earn eighty cents to every male dollar is because we're reluctant to ask for that extra twenty cents.

Of course, it was never about the money. You didn't study English lit because you intended to make millions of dollars. You didn't join the Peace Corps because you thought it would be a shrewd career move.

But just because money isn't your first motivator, it doesn't mean you don't deserve to get paid what you're worth.

You tend to undervalue the experience you've earned over time, and the insights that experience grants you. When something seems obvious to you, you don't necessarily see the value in it.

Sometimes you will be the only woman in the room, and early on you may equate a difference in your perspective with it lacking worth. Don't do that. Have confidence: Often the other people in the room don't even realize they're missing something.

So stop holding your tongue. Own your perspective, insights, recommendations, and ideas. Other people's opinions might be worth less... but because they have the confidence to ask, they get paid more.

So keep giving. Keep carrying on. Keep getting the job done.

Just stop along the way to remind yourself of the value you're providing. Understand what you're worth. And then take a deep breath and ask for it.

Jen.

AFTER A TWO-YEAR STINT ON AN EAST AFRICAN ISLAND AS A Peace Corps volunteer, followed by a junior-editor gig at a start-up magazine, JENNIFER STEVENS crashed a cocktail party and landed a job with Agora's flagship publication, International Living. She has now been editing and writing editorial and direct mail copy for twenty-five years, and is today the chief copywriter and executive editor for *International Living.*

❧ 2 ❧

LORRIE MORGAN

∾

"What lies behind us and what lies before us are tiny matters compared to what lies within us."
— *RALPH WALDO EMERSON*

DEAR LORRIE,

Remember when you discovered copywriting in 1999? The Internet had just started to become a shade of what it is today. And you were desperately looking for a way to work from home, so you could spend more time with your sons.

You would never have believed it back then, but a lot of people ended up reading your copy and looked to you for career (and life) advice. I know, it's hard to believe now, but it's true.

You actually became one of the first female copywriters in the info-marketing industry. (Someday, you'll be happy to see so many women joining in the field.) But at the time, you were a something of a pioneer when it came to emotional response copy... especially for selling to women. Legends like John

Carlton, Dan Kennedy and Gary Halbert even considered you a peer, working with you on programs to sell to their fans.

The fact is, you became touted as a guru for females in the marketing space. You ended up running events, seminars and courses. You taught thousands of people all over the world how to become copywriters and marketers.

But as you come up on the twentieth anniversary of your entry into copywriting, you will want to give it all up.

You will want to get a regular job. You will want a quiet little life that avoids as many people as possible, so you don't have to talk about all the ways you're failing—in your marriage, in your business, in yourself.

By 2016 your second marriage will be so stressful that you will barely eat for a year. You'll live on Ensure (a meal replacement used for old people who can't chew their food). You'll drag yourself through the days, and try to convince yourself that you've had a good enough life, so it's okay to settle for misery.

As a last-ditch effort to give yourself a kickstart, you will sink months of hard labor and over $10,000 into building a course that will not create a cent in revenue. Not one single penny. You will hit rock bottom. And that's what you'll need.

Next, things will start to get brighter again. It's at this point that you will realize that the universe is moving—and something was very misaligned in your life. You get to make different choices.

And the moment you do, a light will switch on and bring you back to yourself. In that moment, choosing to meet your own needs regardless of what others think, you will realize that you don't have to stay where you are.

It will suddenly become clear that you don't have to be miserable. You CAN take care of yourself. And you have a lot of options in front of you.

Best of all, you will remember who you are, and realize (not for the first time) that self-love has to come from within. No one else can validate you; you have to trust yourself and learn that it's okay to do what's right just for you.

You are the only person you have to please. If you're happy then your choices are right.

So, remember who you are. Remember that you are the only one who can create the life you want. You are the only one who can share your gifts with the world. Sometimes you might still get into a bad frame of mind. That's okay. You're only human. So here are some techniques to shift yourself back into greatness:

TAKE CARE OF YOURSELF FIRST.

It's so easy to let clients, colleagues, friends and family dictate how you will prioritize your day. Don't put off what feeds you. Schedule in YOUR time first. Be sure you schedule in exercise, healthy meals, and fun time. You can't be creative if you are just working, working, working.

OWN IT, BABY.

No matter what you wear or how you feel, throw your shoulders back, stand up straight and smile. When we physically act "as if" we are all that and a bag o' chips, our mind starts believing it too.

(You can use this technique when you're working out and feeling exhausted, too—try smiling and tightening up your form. Before you know it, you'll have an added burst of energy.) So fake it till you make it!

BANISH CRITICISM.

How to put this delicately... I've been told, "Opinions are like a-holes. Everybody has one". Now, constructive criticism is very much appreciated. You must know what is and isn't working with your market. But you may be surprised at the barrage of nasty, pointless emails gurus get when they put their work out into the world.

Just be sure all criticism is filtered through an assistant, or trusted advisor, who knows how to help. Do not run your business by committee.

DON'T RESPOND EMOTIONALLY.

In our instant world of email and instant messaging, it's very easy to react to something you don't like. It takes a much bigger person to sit with an issue and respond professionally—later.

If something pushes your buttons, give it at least twenty-four hours. Then you can respond with a cool head and not leave an embarrassing trail of actions you wish you could 'do over.'

YOU'RE COOL. WE KNOW IT.

Sometimes you have to remind yourself how awesome you really are. Take fifteen minutes and write out thirty successes you have had over your lifetime—no matter how big or small.

Tap dance in a recital at three years old? Put it in. Launched your blog? Put it in. Closed a client? Put it in. Add everything you can think of, whether personal or business. Then post it where you will see it often.

WHAT ELSE ARE YOU DOING?

It's not just about the here and now. Think BIG. What do you have planned for the rest of your life? Write down your top twenty big picture goals and look at them regularly. Don't worry about how they will happen. Just focus on what they are. What you focus on expands, so as you look at your goals regularly, don't be surprised if they seem to magically happen.

BE POSITIVE.

You know about affirmations (positive statements you say to your subconscious to visualize the outcome you want for your future), but are you using them daily?

Write them on Post-it notes stuck around your office and bathroom mirror. Create a list that you recite first thing each day. Remember to say your affirmation as if you already have it using the present tense. Things like, "I am confident, organized, and self- assured."

ATTITUDE OF GRATITUDE.

It is impossible to feel truly grateful for what you have and constricted in the same moment. Each morning and evening think of ten things you're grateful for. You will feel your state of mind shift when you're grateful for what is already in your life.

You can't operate at FULL MOJO if you're not firing on all magnificent cylinders. Tap into that greatness that is in you. Then get out there and MAKE A DIFFERENCE! I love you!

LOVE,

Lo

~

LORRIE MORGAN IS CONSIDERED AN INDUSTRY trailblazer in the world of emotional response copywriting and marketing. She founded her first company Red Hot Copy in 1999 an effort to work anywhere, raise her family, and still make a good living.

After studying closely with legends Dan Kennedy, John Carlton, and Gary Halbert, she takes established marketing formulas and added her own conversational rapport to the mix for proven increases in conversions.

Lorrie and her businesses have been featured in Dan Kennedy's Gold Membership, Copy Chief, AWAI (American Writers & Artists Institute), John Carlton's SWS (Simple Writing System), Mal Emery's Business School in Australia, Ladies Who Launch, Office Depot, NAWBO (National Association for Women Business Owners), Mark Victor Hansen's Mega Events and more.

Today Lorrie lives in a rural western town in Southern California with her fiance, her dog and her horses.

LORI HALLER

~

That does not work for me.

DEAR YOUNGER LORI,

Your love for deeply investigating everything around you began early in life. Ocean waves, seashells, music, patterns, colors, books and the glowing moon at night became your family.

Art was your pacifier. It still is.

Learning to write the alphabet and putting letters next to each other gave you goosebumps.

The look of a lower-case "g" hanging far beneath the other letters, and the "t" and "k" standing so tall and majestic made you swoon.

You took these passions and rolled them into a memorable thirty-year design career. Your dreams of owning a successful business and helping others learn and grow came true, and I am so proud of you!

Countless people on your journey were always right there, guiding you with endless love, help and support, giving you everything you needed to succeed.

You fell several times along the way but your "fierce" always pulled you back up. It still does.

And along the way you learned something incredibly important. One little phrase; six words that changed your life forever:

"That does not work for me."

These words might sound or look small on their own, but when you first strung them together as a meaningful reply, they changed your situation completely, and had a huge impact on your life. They still do.

You used these words when a long-time client asked you to create another design for one of their products. The copy would be coming in long past the deadline, which meant that you would not have the time you really needed to create a piece of work you would feel proud to put your name on.

In a moment of clarity and trust, you simply said "No. That does not work for me."

The client heard your words, trusted them and took note of your boundary. They extended the schedule so that you could do your very best work. Instead of creating a conflict, those words built deeper trust and a better outcome for both of you. The campaign ended up being another huge success and the client has continued to hire you, because you know what it takes to do great work.

Those six little words changed your life, and they work just as well in your personal relationships too. You won't believe the impact they can have, so don't be afraid to use them!

Love, sunshine, hope, peace and calm,

Lori

~

LORI HALLER IS AN IN-DEMAND GRAPHIC DESIGNER, speaker, consultant, strategist and team trainer. Besides appearing throughout the United States she also works with several teams abroad.

Lori and her team have been creating award-winning, sales-generating direct mail, space advertising, online promotions and design for more than twenty years. Her agency uses strategy, psychology, technology, behavioral studies, scientific background, research, proven processes and methodologies to create long-running campaigns for a variety of industries.

She has designed magazines, logos, branding, premiums, newsletters, ads, magalogs, mailings, brochures, package design, emails, websites, landing pages, funnels, renewals, books, cookbooks and all manner of products.

Her clients include such prestigious names as Hyatt Hotels, Kay Jewelers, Forbes, The Motley Fool, Agora, Oprah Winfrey's Harpo Productions, Ask Dr. Nandi, and National Geographic.

View her client list and details at: www.lorihaller.com

❧ 4 ❧

LYN MARLER

~

Just because you can be self-sufficient doesn't mean you have to go it alone.

HI, TWENTY-SIX-YEAR-OLD LYN,

You're all set for the airport! You never thought you'd ever go on an adventure like this.

Over the next few years, you'll become the 'overseas relocation expert' for your young family. You'll live in San Diego, Toronto, St. Louis, Tampa, and Sydney... not quite an army wife, but someone has to hold the fort, so you'll choose to be a stay-at-home mum.

All the travel sounds amazing, and it is, but you are shy. Your exposure to a truckload of new people will start to drain you, and eventually it will dig away at your self-esteem. You'll want to crawl under a rock and hide.

It's not that you're a misfit among strangers, but you take on too much. You lock away every conversation you have with someone in your mind, memorizing every detail. You feel it's an important part of caring... but you overwhelm yourself. Many people you meet won't even remember your name, so stop setting the bar so high.

Your future friends, Dennis and Nicki, will nudge you stop making things so difficult on yourself before the urge to become a hermit overwhelms you. You will remember what they tell you for years:

"You've gotta get out of your own way when you meet people, Lyn. When you do, they're drawn in because they see you're engaged and insightful. They know you really care about them. You, young lady, light up people's day."

When you dig for the brave part of yourself and start networking, the insight Dennis and Nicki shared will be spot on. Thank goodness they insisted on getting to know you in spite of yourself!

Be yourself. That's enough. You've got so much empathy that it sometimes weighs you down, but you'll realize it's one of the things you like most about yourself: you're shy, but you still love to be around people, so it's up to you to find people you can relate to.

Try not to be scared. Your self-worth is relying on you, Little Lyn. Give yourself permission to find the handful of people in those huge groups that you actually like. Don't get discouraged if you don't meet the 'friends of your dreams' immediately, because you will find them, and they'll be worth the wait.

Let yourself open up to them, and realize that just because you can be self-sufficient doesn't mean you have to go it alone.

Safe travels...

Lyn in her fifties.

P.S. When your husband offers to teach you basic computer technology, let him. Don't stick your head in the sand. Don't be stubborn—it's not that hard. You are smarter than you think, and if you do this, you'll find you can have it all... the creative career you love and being a stay-at-home mom!

❧

BEFORE BECOMING A COPYWRITER, LYN MARLER WAS A network marketer and an affiliate of an internet marketing training product. She learned many forms of marketing online and offline including PPC, blogging, press releases, email autoresponders, social media, online classified ads, SEO and much more. She was so passionate about mastering advertising skills that she traveled to twenty-one marketing conferences in a four-year period.

Lyn has taken her training to the next level by studying advanced copywriting with American Writers & Artists Inc. (AWAI). They're recognized as the world's leading online training company for copywriting. She's also passed their verification exam, which means she understands the components of superior sales copy.

Lyn loves exploring your unique business and writing upbeat copy for you that converts. Mostly, she writes online copy and content for lifestyle and travel.

You can reach Lyn and view her samples at www.lynmarler.com

❦ 5 ❦

BILLYE TZIPORAH ROBERTS

∿

Let me tell you what kind of person you are.

DEAR YOUNGER ME,

Your twenties haven't been your best decade and this isn't your best night.

You are bleeding from the cuts on your wrists—up and down, not across—sitting in warm water to help the blood flow. You always could follow instructions, even about the correct way to cut your wrists.

But right now, you're not happy about having followed them. You're crying. You took a bunch of pills because you thought it would help you deal with the physical pain. You really don't like pain. It hurts.

But worse than that is the pain the Crazy inflicts on you every day. He says a lot of horrible and untrue things to you— every time you're alone, every time you are about to fall asleep, every free moment.

The Crazy is pretty happy right now, sitting in the upper

right corner of the room where he always is. He's telling you that you will be better off dead, and that the world will be better off too.

"Besides," he says, *"it's easier. Just give up. Why keep fighting it? You're fat. You're ugly. You're useless. You're worthless. You're stupid. You're using up air more deserving people could be breathing. Even your mother doesn't love you. What kind of a person is it that even a mother doesn't love?"*

Well, let me tell you what kind of person you are.

You are the kind or person who will live through this, even though you will have the scars all your life. You will look at them from time to time, and be so grateful this didn't work. You have a lot to do in this world.

You're the kind of person who is valuable.

You're not working much right now, and you're not sure what you want to do 'when you grow up,' but there will be one year you will earn a salary of $100,000, working a job you are exceptionally good at. It's only fair to mention that your boss is horrible, which is why it only lasts a year, but you will always have a job and manage to support yourself. That is no small thing.

You're the kind of person who is clever.

You will teach yourself about relational databases, HTML coding, CSS and WordPress. You will become a power user of Excel; teach yourself QuickBooks; and to read business Spanish and French. Read that first sentence again. You will teach yourself.

You will have three articles you write published online, and three in print. One will be a high point of your life because it will be published on a huge Jewish website. You will write some incredibly dirty fan fiction, which you will be way too ashamed to share with anyone except one friend. She is going to completely confuse you by telling you she likes them.

You will be an officer at the city, state and multi-state level of an international medieval reenactment group (the Society for Creative Anachronism—the SCA). You haven't heard of it yet, but the people in this organization believe in living a Dream where Honor and Service are upmost. You don't know this yet either, but you will believe that too. And you will deserve, and receive, their highest award for organization and service.

You're the kind of person who is resourceful and curious.

You will drive across the U.S. by yourself three times. You'll go to England, Scotland and the Continent. You will live in Texas, California, Colorado, Virginia, Pennsylvania, and Maryland; and you will own two houses in Colorado, and one (the dream house that will, unfortunately, get away) in Virginia.

You will continue to pursue your quest to answer the questions about the Universe you feel when you are dancing with the sea, or watching what you will call the Tits of God (the Rocky Mountains) when they are looking so beautiful you think they must be illustrated. You will become a second-degree Wiccan High Priestess, and later, you will convert to Judaism. You will continue to care deeply about the meaning of "life, the Universe and everything," even after you know Douglas Adams found the answer, and it's "42."

You're the kind of person who is a blessing to others.

You will create and run a project to make quilts for a women's homeless shelter, and you will organize others to take food—and take food yourself—to that same shelter for ten years. For three years you will organize and serve Christmas meals to three hundred men at a homeless shelter.

You will never have children of your body, but your 'kids' will be the folks you help get their start in the SCA, and your godchildren. They will all outdo your achievements by leaps and bounds and that will make you proud.

That's the kind of person you are.

Know that this 'sincere, but not serious' attempt to kill yourself (as a psychiatrist friend will put it) is going to create a door. You will walk through it and once you get to the other side, suicide will never again be an option for solving your problems. Your Crazy will slowly fade away.

I'm not going to tell you your life will be perfect. It won't be. I've mentioned some of the glitches already; another is that you will leave a good man who loves you. You are going to "pay the price for the chains your refuse," as Richard Thompson put it in Beeswing.

Everything has a price. You will make choices along the way about the prices you are willing to pay. You won't always be right. But you'll still be here, fifty years later. And in the main, you will have few regrets.

So get out of that tub of cooling water. Tape up your wrists and sleep off the drugs.

You are not going to die today.

You are going to live to do something world changing. You are going to live to help a lot of people. Surviving tonight's pain will be worth it.

You are going to change the world. You are about to write a book that will help start to eliminate homelessness among women.

Yes, you are having a rock bottom, lousy night. But remember, you've got that list of things you've going to make happen. The Universe intends you to help a lot of people, and even without the list, that's more than enough to balance out everything else—even the scars.

Never trust anyone who says "trust me." But... *trust me* on this.

Love,
The Older You

~

BILLYE TZIPORAH ROBERTS LIVES IN THE DMV (DC, Maryland, Virginia). As much as she has always wanted to write and to help people, she realized recently she has spent the last

35

ten years at a cruise control sort of job. What she really wants to do is change the world with her writing. She's decided to get on that. Other pertinent info: No husband, no kids, no pets, lots of quilts.

You can see her current writing at www.hevria.com/billye

❦ 6 ❦

LAURA GALE

∿

The only standard you have to hold is your own.

LAURA,

One warm night in February, when you're 19 years old, you'll marshall what's left of your energy and force your way out of the room your lover locked you in. Bruised, bleeding, you'll tear down the drive, praying to make the car before the house wakes up.

Running, you'll see all at once that no one could have saved you. You trusted the wrong people; all this time, you've been praying to yourself. And in the moment the engine turns over, that accursed house will erupt behind you, and you'll be gone.

Driving, your body is remade. You become unbreakable, electric in the knowledge that within you is everything you'll ever need. All was lost; all is just beginning.

In the years that follow, the self-reliance forged that night will scare people. They'll say you're hard, cold, distant. They'll say you come on too strong, you're too intense, you expect an impossible standard.

But others will look into that dark stillness and see themselves reflected there. They recognize your ambition and clarity, because it's theirs too. Those are your people, and they'll love you for your sharp edges. You'll help each other reach new frontiers, and together you'll find that fun and joy and wonder are not incompatible with seeking growth and wisdom.

Your self-reliance will put you in the room with some of the best minds of your generation, and with the legends that raised them. As you trust yourself, so others will learn to trust you, and you'll be humbled by the knowledge and wisdom so many incredible people entrust to your care.

Remember, though, that self-reliance can also be a very effective shield. For years, it will protect you from feeling or fearing too deeply. In time, you will have to learn to lower it enough to let people love you. Sometimes it's good to rely on others too.

Refuse to carry others' angst. Their choices are theirs; the only standard you have to hold is your own. Don't fear loneliness, though it's coming; joy is coming too. Banish that thief, comparison, always whispering that you should be smaller, more obedient, more like the other girls.

When you're under pressure, remember that stillness. Go into it as often as you need. Hold your shield up, or let it down, but whatever you do, trust yourself. You're strong, built for taking big swings, and every swing creates a momentum that quietly, profoundly changes everything.

And remember through it all that you are enough, you are worthy, you are enough, and you already have everything within you that you will ever need.

Laura.

~

LAURA GALE IS A GHOSTWRITER AND DEVELOPMENTAL editor, specializing in book development for business owners.

Born and raised in Sydney, Australia, she now lives in Lisbon, Portugal. She has a degree in writing and publishing, and got her start in publishing working on projects like the *Twilight* phenomenon, JK Rowling's post-*Harry Potter* publications, and the memoirs of Michael Palin, Nelson Mandela and Tina Fey. Now she helps entrepreneurs and direct response marketers to create books that transform their businesses. Laura is also the bestselling author of *Content That Converts* and *How To Write This Book*.

www.lauraiswriting.com

NOT-SO-SECRET
LESSON #2

NEVER TRADE YOUR AUTHENTICITY FOR EASE OR SAFETY

∼

Sometimes it's just easier to pretend to be someone or something you're not. Sometimes it's easier to fake it until you fit in. Sometimes it's easier to swallow the words you really want to say, and just play the game. We've all done it—pretended to be different to make things easier on ourselves, to avoid rocking the boat, or because we think it's what's necessary to be successful. But when you hide who you really are, eventually you end up paying a price— and the cost is always too high.

Popular researcher and TED speaker Dr. Brené Brown warns that when you trade your authenticity for safety, you can end up anxious, depressed and even addicted. You may find yourself suffering from unexplained grief, resentment and rage. In other words, if you're not careful you'll end up mad as hell with a bottle of bourbon sobbing over the latest episode of *This Is Us* on Netflix.

All of the women in this chapter spent years hiding their true selves until the price became too high. As Jen puts it, "You can only be a method actor for so long before you go utterly mad."

Growing up in small-town Nebraska, she is conditioned to

build a life that she believes other people will approve of and understand—even though it isn't the life that she wants. Ilise is terrified to let on that she doesn't understand, so she nods and pretends to be something she is not. Pam doesn't believe she can be a technology geek *and* creative. She spends her days trapped in a corporate cubicle dreaming of a more creative life. Dawn is afraid to admit she no longer wants the Hollywood dream even though she's spent her entire youth chasing it. And Hillary hides her "enormous Godzilla of a personality" because she believes she has to be like all the other girls to succeed in her work.

For each of these Titanides, there comes a time when they cannot pretend anymore, when they must become 'real'. It's when these daring women finally let their authentic selves shine and their 'Geek flags fly' that they find success in business and in life. So if you've been trading your authenticity for safety, maybe it's time to take a deep breath, put down the bourbon, and start walking down your own road.

1

JEN ADAMS

~

You can only be a method actor for so long before you go utterly mad.

HELLO DARLING,

You do you, okay?

Now, I know that's not what you're about to do.

Instead, you're about to take the adventurous, travel-filled life that you love... and throw it all away.

I forgive you. Eventually, you'll forgive yourself, too.

You see, when you get back to the place where your life is something you deeply enjoy again, you will need to have taken the hard road to truly appreciate how lovely and amazing things can be when you're being yourself.

But let's get back to the start of that hard road...

When you graduated from university with your dual degree, your parents half-hoped you'd go into the foreign service. That crash course in teaching English and the job in Japan were a bit of a rebellion.

So, too, was the impulsive move to Shanghai. All those fabulous people... the ones your grandmother would later refer as

45

your "bohemian friends in the Orient"... gifted you with a lifetime's worth of stories. Yet layered on top of it all was the pressure. No one in your family—almost all lawyers, bankers, and accountants—could understand why teaching overseas was 'all you wanted' from your life.

Over time, that pressure is going to get to you. You've been too different for too long. When your roommate in Shanghai is accepted into Wharton's business program, you take it as a cosmic hint that it's finally time to get a 'real' job.

So you're going to take a turn at building a life you think other people will approve of and understand.

You don't realize it at first, but you have made yourself very interesting to American employers. You get into one of the top three HR programs in the country, and companies like Microsoft and G.E. fly you all over for interviews. You get a fancy job at Bank of America in their talent development department... and by the second day, you know you've made a terrible mistake.

But how can you walk away after they have paid to relocate you, and when your family finally understands what you're doing?

You were conditioned for the first two decades of your life to be a conformist and a people-pleaser. It came with the territory living in small-town Nebraska, and while you know it's not who you really are, you haven't yet developed the confidence you need to embrace that truth and let your real self shine.

So you're going to try very hard to be someone you're not. And you'll succeed for a time. You'll have every outward appearance of having your act together.

But you'll feel like a hot mess on the inside. Which, by the way, is perfectly okay and perfectly valid. You can only be a method actor for so long before you go utterly mad.

Despite the inner turmoil, you won't sacrifice this show of being 'normal' voluntarily. After everything you've invested— time, energy, shares of your soul—you're going to need a hard push from the universe to break free.

It will come in 2008 when the financial markets crash. As the crisis unfolds, your HR team will win awards for how fast you fire people. Then you'll be shown the door yourself. This will seem like a terrible setback to the regular folks around you... but all you feel is relief. The curtain is finally down and the whole show is over.

You start writing in earnest, and soon you're making enough money that no one will ever be able to drag you back onto that stage again.

And now... now you get to stand up and start spreading your wings. Your polite resistance and Emily Post no-thank-yous will give way to loud hell-nos, middle finger waved proudly at the world of ought-to and should-do.

Eventually, the world will get the hint.

You're not what they want you to be.

You're not going to be what they think is appropriate, suitable, or even understandable.

You're going to be something else. Independent, entrepreneurial, coloring outside of the lines.

But you wouldn't be here if you hadn't gone through that soulless corporate phase of it all. That detour gave you a fluency in the business world you wouldn't have otherwise, and that you have needed so frequently in the return to this lovely life—the free-roaming, freelance adventure your family doesn't fully understand.

So live through it, darling. Give yourself a little grace and milk the experience for all it's worth. Because when the time comes, you'll be ready to take a deep breath, stand up straight, and start walking down your own road.

You do you. You're the only one who can.

Much love,

Your future.

JEN ADAMS WAS BORN AND RAISED IN NEBRASKA. SHE STILL

firmly believes there's nothing as beautiful as the rolling prairie... for a visit. Currently based in Lansing, MI, she's spent most of her adult life traveling, living by turns in Asia, Europe, and South America.

Jen writes long-form sales letters and email copy for clients in the financial, health, personal development, and lifestyle niches. She's a founding partner of the Titanides and serves as Managing Editor for AWAI's Professional Writers' Alliance.

In her free time ... hahahahaha. Free time. You're funny. When she's not writing, Jen serves as "parent on point" for her two small boys and "queen of logistics" for her husband, an audio engineer and composer. To connect with her online, ping her on LinkedIn: http://bit.ly/2xU8X7D

❦ 2 ❦

PAM FOSTER

~

Embrace your geekiness. It has tremendous value.

DEAR PAM IN 1987,

You are a Geek Goddess. *(This is not a typo! Not Greek Goddess.)*

I have come to learn that being a geek is an incredible gift for you.

Just know that when you're hanging out with your beloved artsy friends and wistfully admiring their abilities to paint, sculpt, create gorgeous photographs, and so on... you shouldn't feel left out.

There's plenty of room for creative types (you) who are also quite geeky (you). You belong in a world that accepts and even celebrates both!

You will grow up with the Web, and evolve with the technology.

Your skills—your writing, your understanding of the user experience, your ability move people through a site, and your love of SEO—are paramount to how marketing will work in the future. Your role at a veterinary technology company will give you plenty of opportunity to practice geeking out on all things Internet.

But by the end of 2005, you will want out of the corporate confines that have started chafing at you, especially once the company starts reorganizing every few months.

One winter day you will get home at 4 p.m.—when it's pitch black out, cold and miserable—and pick up a mailing from Paul Hollingshead at AWAI (American Writers & Artists Inc.). The headline will change your life forever. It says:

RETIRE THIS YEAR!

And Still Make More Money Than Most Doctors...

It's all about freelance copywriting. Immediately, you will see that this is it! This is your 'out'. You can finally plan to leave corporate cubicles behind. Best of all, your company will pay for you to attend your first AWAI Copywriting Bootcamp, and soon you'll be implementing everything you learned to get some successful campaigns under your belt.

And when you marshall your courage and tell your company you're ready to go out on your own, you don't burn your bridges. Your former employer, recognizing the power of the geek in you, will become your first client.

As you start freelancing, a weight will lift off you as you enter a community of people who get to live and work the way you want to live and work... and who WANT you to be creative AND geeky.

They know that when it comes to writing effective copy you have to be able to blend creative problem-solving, persuasive writing, and super geeky SEO techniques.

So embrace your geekiness. Have fun with it! It has tremendous value.

If you can embrace your geeky gifts, you'll discover that you can:

- Weave a magical blend with your web copywriting,

bringing throngs of customers to your clients' websites.

- Speak geek with the best of the programming/IT nerds who hire you to work on websites. (They'll respect and appreciate your geekiness!)
- Be one of the best at writing about B2B gizmos in ways that strike the emotions of prospects while nurturing their need for clarity and logic.
- Create training programs that offer practical, nerdy, step-by-step guidance while entertaining recipients and encouraging their successes. You will be a fun geek teacher!

Finally, you'll find a proud, inclusive and loving sisterhood of fellow female geeks, such as Heather Lloyd-Martin, C.S. Wurzburger, Margot Howard, and many, many others.

Never be afraid to let your geek flag fly!

Love,

Pam

PAM FOSTER IS THE DIRECTOR OF COPYWRITING Training at AWAI and also the owner of ContentClear Marketing. As a Certified SEO Copywriter, she enjoys helping clients with her unique blend of smart copywriting and geeky keyword use. She's apt to burst into song at any moment, and she tries to find the humor in most situations and make people smile. She also loves organizing stuff, creating outlines and checklists, hosting potluck gatherings, learning geeky things, and teaching people how to thrive.

Visit her at www.awaionline.com/bio/pam-foster, www. contentclear.com or www.linkedin.com/in/pamfostercontentclear for more.

ILISE BENUN

∽

To be guided, you must trust.

DEAR YOUNG ILISE,

They say youth is wasted on the young, and I do think that's true. You were young, impetuous and arrogant, and you had no idea what you were doing. For that you are forgiven.

But if there is an opportunity to learn from your mistakes, here is my advice:

Don't pretend. Don't pretend to be something you're not, to know something you don't or to understand things that make no sense to you.

Before you found your niche working with creative professionals, you came across all kinds of people doing things you didn't understand. You purported to be able to help them—even though you had no idea what they needed—just because you didn't want them to know that you didn't get it.

There's no reason to pretend and worse, it can be very damaging. There were plenty of mistakes you could have avoided, and opportunities you could have taken advantage of, if you hadn't been so afraid to let on that you didn't understand. Instead you nodded as if you did. You weren't fooling anyone.

Get help. Don't go it alone. We all have to have our own experiences, but we don't have to make all the mistakes. Allow yourself to be open to guidance, and admit when you need some outside perspective. Good guidance—from someone with real experience—is priceless and worth every penny. It will save you years of error.

However, to be guided, you must trust. Not everyone, of course, but the decent ones, who have no stake in your success and actually just want to help you. That means you have to open your eyes, to be vigilant and exercise quality control over what gets in and what doesn't.

Focus on learning. Growing up you were told that you could do anything you wanted, but you weren't told that you would need to learn what you were doing *first*, before you would get what you wanted.

This is universal to your whole life, not just your work. It will become clear that you have a lot to learn on many levels, and that learning is everything.

Nothing else matters. Your biggest client doesn't matter. Writing books doesn't matter. Speaking engagements don't matter. The only goal should be to learn from every experience, and then move on to better.

And of course, it's never too late to learn any of these things.

Good luck.

Ilise Benun

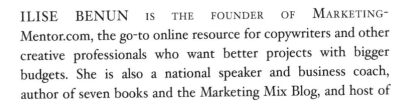

ILISE BENUN IS THE FOUNDER OF MARKETING-Mentor.com, the go-to online resource for copywriters and other creative professionals who want better projects with bigger budgets. She is also a national speaker and business coach, author of seven books and the Marketing Mix Blog, and host of the Marketing Mentor Podcast. She teaches as adjunct faculty at Maryland Institute College of Art. Her online courses can also be found through CreativeLive, HOW Design University and American Writers & Artists Institute. She is also Program Partner for HOW Design Live. Follow her @ilisebenun and get her Quick Tips: www.marketing-mentortips.com

❧ 4 ❧

DAWN EASON

~

You built your young life around this dream, but it will turn out to be the wrong dream.

DEAR DAWN,

You will be twelve years old when you start modeling and acting. You have been angling for this since you were five, but your mother is the opposite of the stage moms you used to hear about. She will tell you for *years* that you need to be older to really understand what you are getting into.

You think you *do* know, and you are so impatient to get started! When you finally convince her to start taking you to auditions, she will drive you into the city from the suburbs for months, taking you to every audition, even when you get rejected over and over and over again.

After so many rejections, a stage manager will tell you that if you really want to do this, you need to hone your craft. You will need to take acting lessons and voice lessons, and you need to learn how to work with photographers and directors.

She will tell you that this process—learning the craft,

practicing for the love of it—will make all the difference. So you will do as she said, and practice until you get your first agent.

But by the time you are sixteen, you will have a secret.

After all the work, all the practice, you won't love it. You won't even like it. You built your young life around this dream, but it will turn out to be the wrong dream.

Acting is so hard for you. You are so sensitive emotionally, and leaning into all the pain and struggle of a character upsets you deeply. Even when you start getting great parts, you won't feel empowered in your abilities, and it will start to affect your confidence.

But you can't tell anyone. This is what you have wanted for so long! This was what your mother gave up her time for. This is what you have been working at tirelessly for *years*, while the other girls your age are having their middle school fun.

And isn't this the dream? Doesn't everyone want this? Your friends are so jealous.

You get to be famous. You can make so much money. You live such a glamorous life.

In 1990 you land a part on a new show called *Hull High*, billed as the TV version of *Fame*. You arrive on set, and the assistant director comes over to sign you in. He gives you the schedule for the day, tells you where to be and when, and says he will be back to take you to hair and make-up in ten minutes. He is in charge, and everyone knows it.

As he walks away, you think, *"I want be the guy with the clipboard!"*

But that thought is dangerous, and in the same moment, you think, *"I can't tell anyone that. I'm not supposed to be the guy with the clipboard."*

Later that day, when you finally get on set, you convince the director to let you yell *"Action!!"*

You get a huge rush from it, like nothing you have experienced before, and it scares you so much that you never tell a soul and put all those dangerous ideas out of your head.

Seven years later you will go to Australia to film *Roar* with Heath Ledger. During the auditions, you will ask so many questions about how the show was going to run that the producer, Sean Cassidy, sees that dangerous idea that is buried so deep inside you.

He will call a mutual friend, a script writer, and tell her that you are no actress—you are a producer. He saw straight through you, and all your hopes come rushing back.

And when you marry Bo a year later, you get your big chance to become the producer you had secretly wished you could be.

When Bo finished writing his play, *Runt of the Litter*, you found someone to type the script, you showed up to every rehearsal, you ran the lights and even engineered the sound for the play. As it went on tour all over the country, you got to put on a production, to entertain and create an amazing experience for the audience—and you didn't have to spend a second on stage.

You got to have creative control, you got to work with some incredibly talented people, and you got to create a safe environment for Bo to perform at his best.

In time, you will get to do the same for people all over the country. When you and Bo start Personal Story Power, you will get to create the same safe environment and amazing experiences for entrepreneurs, leaders and and professionals who want to learn to tell their stories in a powerful, authentic way.

These days, Bo is always telling audiences that you are like a grizzly bear. You have been fighting for his dream, for our dream, for the past eighteen years, and now we fight for other people's dreams too. Your ability to connect deeply with people, to understand what they need in each moment to deliver their best, is a core part of how you fight on their behalf.

Twenty-six years ago, you were a sixteen-year-old actress on a set in Hollywood, living the wrong dream. Today, far more than being just someone with a clipboard, you are a world-class producer, living the dream that you were made for.

Dawn.

~

DAWN EASON BEGAN AS AN ACTRESS AND WAS WELL KNOWN for her recurring role on television's *Melrose Place*. Her career as a producer began in 2001 with *Runt of the Litter*, which was named one of the top off-Broadway plays of 2002.

Along with producing the play's national tour, Dawn is currently producing the feature film of *Runt of the Litter* with Frank Darabont (writer/director of *The Shawshank Redemption* and *The Green Mile*).

As Managing Partner of The Bo Eason Experience, Dawn runs operations for the company's ten live events, manages Bo Eason's speaking commitments, and helps develop and present digital and print material to create the superior quality of experience that the company's coaching and workshop clients have come to expect.

Even before their marriage in 1998, Bo and Dawn had formed a dynamic partnership whose mission today is to help others tap the power of their personal story and become effective, persuasive communicators. Dawn and Bo live in Southern California and have three children, Eloise, Axel and Lyla Bo.

5

HILLARY WEISS

~

You're not going to show up if you're bored to death.

DEAR HILLARY,

You're twenty-two! So young to be starting a business. You're going to go a long way in the next few years, and I want you to know a few things.

THING #1:

It is okay to take yourself seriously. You are very *unserious* in the grand scheme of things, but it's so important to take your values and strengths seriously. Women are so prone to apologize for taking up space, for our bigness, for being loud, and it holds us back so much.

So be loud. Take up space. Refuse to shut up. When they tell you to be less, be more.

Because if you want to run a business, you have to allow yourself to get bigger. Not in the sense of letting your ego get out of control, but you have to trust yourself. You have to be who you are and respect your own abilities enough that you can bring the best of yourself to whatever it is you're working on.

It's not until you realize that your enormous Godzilla of a personality could be part of your branding—not something to be hidden—that you'll be able to take steps that are unique in your space, and really get clarity about how you want to show up in your business and in your life.

THING #2:

Take the things you like and turn them into a business. You're not going to show up if you're bored to death.

There is more to building a copywriting business than teaching people the ten key steps to optimizing their sales pages. You watched Alexandra Franzen build her whole business on creating a unique voice and doing things her way rather than relying on advertising. She was so good, because she knew what she did and didn't want, and she knew how to show up for her clients and create experiences that they loved.

You don't have to do it like the other girls that came out of the Public Relations world, all lined up with their soy lattes and neon-cased BlackBerries. You don't have to do it like the other copywriters who only talk about conversions and controls. You don't have to do it like the old-school marketers who tell you that if you want to be respectable and taken seriously that you have to 'play the game' and 'enter the machine' to pay your dues.

So stop writing stuff that you hate writing about, and talk about the stuff that really matters to you. When you realize you can let that shit go, and start writing about stuff that you really care about—like burnout, the nature of entrepreneurship, how niches are changing, how to make people give a damn about you and your work—your business will take off. You'll be more excited to write, your voice will be unique among all the same-same stuff out there, and it will draw the right people into your world.

THING #3:

You are going to burn yourself down to the ground more times than you can count, and this is something you need to get a handle on.

Your instinct has always been just to work harder and harder —you might not be the most talented or the smartest, but you will outwork *everyone*, and that's been the engine that has driven your business forward. But after pushing yourself to the brink of exhaustion so many times, you're going to learn that success no longer comes from pushing and shoving yourself past these big milestones.

You have to get super intentional about where you dedicate your focus. That's an incredibly nebulous thing to work out, but you've come this far—everything is figure-out-able. You're going to work it out one way or another, but getting intentional is the most important thing you can do to break past the next upper limit you're facing.

Being intentional is not about just changing your business model. There are three dimensions to intentionality: doing the work you want to do, with the clients you want to work with, and how you do the work—being mindful of how your time and energy are spent on each project.

You can raise your rates at any time, you can switch your model at any time, you can let clients go. You might know what you don't want, but if you don't get clear on what you do want, there's no roadmap. So instead of making huge shifts as soon as you think you have an answer, write it all down. Map out your vision, get really clear on what you do and don't want (for both your business and your life), *slow down,* and then take the next step.

So, young one, remember that much of building a creative business is about taking swings, and not being afraid to miss. Your mistakes won't kill you; every misfire just shows you where not to shoot. Have the courage to out yourself out there, and to test stuff even if it's not perfect.

Commit to positivity and radical transparency. Have the conversations you want to have, say the things you want to say, do the work you want to do. Follow the fun, and whatever you do, just keep showing up.

Hillary.

~

HILLARY WEISS IS THE CHIEF COPYWRITER, GHOSTWRITER, and mischief-maker over at hillaryweiss.com. Since 2011, she's helped over 150 brands find their voice, and get seen and heard with content that truly speaks their language, and fits their phenomenal work. Because words that lift hearts, ignite minds, and get results can do more than just change your business—they can change the world too.

These days, content's gotta be better than "good". Leading brands create evocative experiences—with smart, succinct phrasing that blasts through the echochamber of our digital universe. So that's what Hillary is here to help you do—with a killer combo of deep listening (to you and your people), keen ears and eyes for innovation, and an unshakeable allergy to ho-hum formulas. It's been her specialty since 2011. And damn, does she love her job.

Wanna know more? Catch her riffs on creativity and the art of writing on her blog, or you say whaddaaap! to her on Twitter @hcweiss.

NOT-SO-SECRET
LESSON #3

DON'T LET SUPER WOMAN KILL YOU

~

It seemed empowering at the time... the second wave of feminism taught women that we could do anything, be anything, and achieve anything we wanted.

All that opportunity was liberating until it became a noose around our necks. Until we started to believe we had to strap on our thigh-high boots and red cape and perform like Super Woman every single day of our lives.

The myth of Super Woman says, *"You can be the best mom, the best wife, the best daughter, the best boss, the best volunteer, the best employee... and you can do it all without breaking a sweat."*

Super Woman convinces you that you must keep doing, doing, doing all the time like Joyce. She tricks you into over-committing, volunteering for every committee, and taking care of everyone else like Lisa. Super Woman wears her busy-ness like a badge of honor and prides herself on always being 'first in, last out' like Rebecca. And Super Woman codes a complex compiler, moves a household while nine months pregnant, and cooks and serves Thanksgiving dinner for dozens like Denise.

If you aren't careful, that Super Woman will kill you. She will force you to keep going, keep pushing, and keep doing, until you break. Until you find yourself like Colleen sobbing at your desk, overtired and overworked and out of fun. Or you find yourself like Renee, facing the same terminal cancer diagnosis that took her mother.

If someday you too find yourself at the breaking point, you will have to choose. You will be forced, as these Titanides were, to finally let go of the myth of Super Woman.

When that time comes, remember how to breathe, deep breaths in and out. Take time to rest, to take care of your body and soul. Practice being still. Take joy in creating. Ask yourself, "What makes me happy?" Then ditch the boots and the cape and admit you're only human after all.

RENEE TELLER

～

You're going to keep getting hit with a more difficult challenge until you stop, or you die.

DEAR RENEE,

You were about four years old when you overheard your grandmother Millie say to your grandfather, *"Art, I'm afraid that Renee is going to be beautiful, but dumb."*

You didn't laugh, you didn't cry. You just decided you would be the smartest, that you would work the hardest. And that's exactly what you did, for the next forty years. You never, for a second, considered slowing down to think about what you actually wanted from your life.

Your career began as a CPA in an international accounting firm. Your husband was in a similar role, and over time the demands of the work—twelve to fifteen hour days for several months of the year—started to take a toll. In order to save your marriage, you took a job in commercial real estate, thinking it wouldn't be so demanding.

But you went from the frying pan into the fire. It was twelve to fifteen hours a day, every day, all year. It was even more male-dominated, more cutthroat than finance had been. Things fell apart in your marriage, but that didn't slow you down.

One rare night, you were home early enough to read your son a bedtime story. He was eight years old, and as you opened the book he looked up at you with his big blue eyes and asked, *"Mommy? Why is there a man with a gun sitting in the living room every night?"*

How do you explain to an eight-year old that Mommy's firm had accidentally hired the Mafia, who had threatened us all with our lives, and so the man in living room was there to protect us from being killed? You realized at that moment that you had put his physical life, and his emotional life, in danger. But that didn't slow you down either.

Soon afterwards your mother was diagnosed with an incurable, untreatable cancer. She had been ten years breast cancer free, and so when she was diagnosed, you knew you had to stop what you were doing. But even then you couldn't slow down.

Within a year you had opened a wellness center. You wanted to teach people that they could never be well if they were not well in body, mind and soul. Your center was open seven days a week, fifteen hours a day—you were teaching thousands to slow down but *you* still didn't slow down.

Finally, it was like the Universe said, *"Okay — if you don't stop and listen, intently, you're going to keep getting hit with a more difficult challenge until you stop, or you die."*

You were diagnosed with that same incurable cancer that took your mom's life.

You never stopped until your life was on the line, but those lessons were God's way of getting you to the spot where you can live your purpose. They were meant to make you to really truly stop, not just slow down.

So Renee: Stop. Listen to your heart and what's going on inside you. And please God, let that be the last lesson.

Get to truly know yourself. The only way to do that is to be still with yourself, *a lot*. You might not feel like you have the right to be still with yourself—our world has made heroes out of workaholics—but if you are ever going to become who you are supposed to be, you need to take that time to be still.

And give yourself more grace. You are allowed to not constantly be reaching and striving for the next summit. Enjoy and understand that the *journey* is what makes living good—not the finish line. There *is* no finish line.

Allow yourself to get out of your head and into your heart, because it's only when you do this that you will be able to become a better version of yourself. You don't have to spend all your energy making sure your grandmother wasn't right anymore.

Of course, that's easier now for you that neuroscience is catching up with the wisdom of the ancient philosophers—that what we repeatedly think about is what we end up building our emotions on, which then leads to all our actions.

Once you realize that the brain is just an organ like your heart and lungs, and can be trained to perform how you want it to, you can stop letting your brain run your life. You will still do all your due diligence, but listening more to your heart will let you rewire the pathways in your brain that have been worn in a little too deep.

So over time you will train your brain. You will take your phone in the morning and set a stopwatch for one minute. You will tell yourself that if you open your eyes before the minute was up, you would have to do another minute. And you won't be able to do it.

At the beginning you will not be able to sit still with yourself for one minute. Your mind will go crazy with everything you have to do, but eventually you will learn to put those thoughts on a little train and let them go by you. That's the starting place, and over time you will learn to sit with yourself.

And as you learn to be still, other things will start to resolve themselves.

Your relationship with your son will blossom. He's a young man now, living in New York City, and you will *so* enjoy who he has become and the relationship you have. You will learn to let go of the regrets over all the time you missed, because he was raised with a nanny, and you will learn to see him as an adult with a full life who enriches yours.

You will learn to communicate to other women just how important this process is—that really taking time to rest goes far beyond getting a massage every now and then. You will start to help women just like you to really get to know themselves. You will help them understand that we are the only ones who can create what we want, and if we don't take the time to discover ourselves we'll never be at peace or find true joy.

And as you settle into this quiet pace, into the stillness, the surgeon treating your renal cell carcinoma will bring you some news. The tumor in your kidney has been misdiagnosed—you do not have the terminal cancer that killed your mother. You have an oncocytoma, a very rare benign tumor that occurs in one percent of all cases. It is completely curable, and you will get a second chance at life.

Today you truly believe that if we don't stop making heroes out of workaholism, if we can't give our leaders and top performers the space they need to truly rest, it will be the demise of the genius, the invention and the creativity that made our country great. History is full of leaders who understood the partnership between work and rest. You're committed to being the best, and that has to include mastering rest.

Be still. I love you.

Renee.

~

RENEE TELLER HELPS MOTIVATED, PROFESSIONAL WOMEN—

the ones who work with such passion that they're nearing the brink of exhaustion—to make the absolute MOST of their lives.

Sometimes this looks like radically changing their work/life balance and majorly up-leveling their health practices. Sometimes it looks like negotiating a far better deal at their current job, in their current profession. Sometimes it looks like jumping ship completely and building their own life raft (and FYI, she helps them turn it into a yacht).

It ALWAYS looks like tuning in to their deepest desires and passions, maximizing (dare she say even exploiting) their God-given talents, and tapping into the highest and truest potential of every woman she works with. It's a thrilling journey, and she is honored to guide women just like you on their paths to greatness.

❦ 2 ❦

JOYCE HOLLMAN

❦

Listening to yourself, you'll become a whole person.

HI THERE, JOYCE!

I sound pretty cheery, I know. That will annoy you, since you're depressed as can be, and wondering what the hell you're doing with your life. You're pretending to be okay, working your job, and trying to get back a guy whose agenda in life is clearly not committing to you.

He's not a bad guy. You think he's what you really want, but he's not what you really need. You're not at the stage yet where you can see past you own desperate need to give, give, give to a man. That's alright. You'll get there, trust me.

Let me reassure you: you will find yourself. And with every passing year, you'll step further and further into the sunlight.

You haven't yet begun to ask yourself what you want in life, who you might be. You've spent your years up until now lost, wandering. Efficient and smart as you are, you've been missing the soft stuff inside.

No, not missing it. Burying it. Burying it deep in the darkness, hoping it won't escape and terrify you. But escape it will. With the help of a warm and wise therapist, you will slowly allow it to seep out.

You'll travel a path that will bring you to Maine, where life is slower and softer than in NYC. You'll marry that guy, controlling everything from the wedding silverware to his schedule.

You'll have two children who are the light of your life. They'll grow up to be amazing, kind, talented people.

And as you learn to take time to get still and listen to your inner voice, you will start to understand what you need from your life. When you stop running around, doing, doing, doing all the time, you will start to hear that small, still voice.

You won't be able to immediately fulfill everything you realize you need, but there will come a day where you can put a stake in the ground and say that the situation is no longer working for you. You'll release yourself from the role of caretaker, and your smarts and your efficiency will stand you in good stead as you finally manage to get divorced.

But smarts won't be all you have anymore. Listening to yourself, you'll become a whole person. And the ability to write, which has saved your soul all these years, will lead you to a career that makes your life and your work one, which you've craved for so long.

Not only that, but writing will lead you to a tribe you can embrace, people who aren't afraid to combine their smarts and their deep emotions. In fact, they make a practice of it. And you'll finally be home.

So don't worry. Every step on the path will be worthwhile, no matter how hard it seems at the time, because it will lead you into the sunlight.

With great love,

Joyce

～

JOYCE HOLLMAN LIVES IN MAINE, AND TAUGHT SPECIAL education for nearly thirty years. After two years of training with AWAI, she left teaching and is now a full-time copywriter in the health and wellness niche. Her training with AWAI is ongoing.

❧ 3 ❧

REBECCA MATTER

~

Life will be far easier if you remind yourself at
every turn that you're doing the best you can.

DEAREST REBECCA,

You're going to be successful. So relax!

I realize the word feels so big and the path in front of you seems overwhelming at times. So I'd like to give you some guidance on how to make that journey more enjoyable.

To start, know that early on, you won't know as much as you think you do. It's going to be a humbling experience after college. But once you figure that out, your real learning can begin.

Surround yourself with smart people. You will have many incredible mentors along the way—be open to every opportunity to learn. Just don't let your ego get in the way. You don't have to know it all, and you won't! So use this time to learn.

Next, be brave.

The best things in life will make you feel like you're going to throw up. I promise they're worth it. Go ahead and walk through every door that opens, and let your heart feast on what it craves.

And finally, practice self-care, both physically and emotionally.

I know you like to burn the candle at both ends, and are proud of your 'first in, last out' way of working. It will come at a cost.

It may seem counterintuitive right now, but the more you can focus on what your body needs—rest, water, sleep—the faster you'll move forward and the more successful you will be.

Remember to BREATHE.

And yes, while being a perfectionist and a strong competitor will serve you well, life will be far easier if you remind yourself at every turn that you're doing the best you can.

And sometimes, most times, that will have to be good enough.

You are good enough. Love you!

Rebecca

REBECCA MATTER IS THE PRESIDENT OF AMERICAN Writers & Artists, Inc. (AWAI), the world's leading trainer of direct-response copywriters. A marketer with two decades of experience in publishing and direct marketing, Rebecca has spearheaded successful million-dollar campaigns for countless products, both online and off, and has spoken and written on topics ranging from getting and working with clients to successful marketing strategies. Rebecca recognizes the tremendous opportunities available to people who know how to write persuasively. She's dedicated herself to keeping AWAI members ahead of the curve... and in demand... by creating cutting-edge programs on the most marketable writing skills today. Connect with her at www.rebeccamatter.com

❧ 4 ❧

LISA CHRISTOFFEL

You'll wear that busy-ness like a badge of honor.
But it isn't.

HEY LISA—HOW YOU DOIN'?

I know the answer to that. You're stressed, overworked, overcommitted, and feeling like your life is out of control. I'm sorry, but you'll have a few more years and some significant ups and downs before you'll find your way back to sanity.

But when you get there, man, it's pretty awesome!

Right now, you've forgotten what you promised yourself a long time ago. You've always had the attitude that you work to live—never that you live to work.

But for the past seven years, you've been working 24x7, missing the boys' birthdays, baseball games, and concerts. Yes, you're moving ahead at your cushy corporate job and making good money, but you're making compromises you'll regret later. It'll all turn out okay, but not without consequences.

Over the next few years, you'll continue to take on way more than you have time for, both with your job and volunteering, and you'll wear that busy-ness like a badge of honor. But it isn't.

You're always the first to raise your hand to help, but you're not helping yourself at all. Every once in a while, you realize what you're doing and you start saying no. Then, as soon as you have balance in your life, you start taking on more and more until you tip yourself into over-commitment all over again.

You'll pay for this, with your health and your happiness. You'll gain over eighty pounds, and you will live in almost constant stress, though you won't realize that until years later. I know you think you're fine. I know you think you're capable of handling everything, and of course you're right: you are.

And then your world will tilt in 2012 when your husband loses his job, and again in 2015, when you lose your job—just after he finally finds one. Your family income will be suddenly and dramatically cut in half, twice, just when the boys start heading to college.

Those life changes are actually the best things that could have happened to you. While you are re-grouping and working to keep your family financially sound, you will wake up and start looking around at how you're living your life, how you're spending your precious time.

You will realize that despite your MBA and your corporate titles, you haven't been as smart as you thought you were.

Don't worry! You will finally take back control: of your income, your time, and your happiness.

When you were younger, you used to write and do all sorts of creative things. But you forgot all about that. Until now. You became a business person and a manager, but you stopped doing creative things. You pursued money and status, but not because you loved what you were doing. There's nothing wrong with money or status, but only if it's acquired through love.

And now that you're doing what you love, you'll be fifty, feeling like you're twenty again.

Now, you're creating again. You're relaxed and happy again.

And you're re-teaching the boys what's really important in life, hopefully before they spend almost fifty years chasing the wrong things.

∾

LISA CHRISTOFFEL IS A FREELANCE COPYWRITER AND THE founder of Christoffel Copywriting, a direct marketing company. She lives with her husband, three boys, one dog and two cats in beautiful upstate NY. She relocated to Rochester twenty-five years ago, but grew up in Pennsylvania, and is a die-hard Nittany Lion and Pittsburgh Steelers fan.

She got her BS degree from Penn State in quantitative business analysis and then her MBA from the Simon School in Rochester in entrepreneurship and finance.

Lisa's middle son now attends Penn State, and she and her husband love heading to Beaver Stadium on game days, getting to see the team and their son. And he loves the free meals he gets when they visit!

Lisa's passions in life have always been her family, her career, and education. She has always loved getting to know people and what made them tick: her company's customers, her fellow volunteers, and the people who worked for her. She gets the greatest joy in helping them improve their skills and attain their goals.

She thinks that's what makes er copywriting more impactful: she takes the time to figure out what prospects need and how your product can solve that need for them. When she switched from a career in service operations to her current career in direct marketing, Lisa spent a considerable amount of time and effort studying and understanding the copywriting business: how to motivate people to take the desired action. She understands direct marketing and how to deliver copy that improves click rates, increases conversions, and builds your customer base.

COLLEEN HAUK

~

What makes me happy?

Dear Colleen,

It's 2013, and tonight is all about the F-word. Yes, it's time you had some F... U... N.

Fun!

You're the working mom you always believed you would be—you've climbed that professional ladder like a pro, and now you're an executive director at a highly coveted digital media company.

But you've been walking around like you're drunk, living on only four hours of sleep each night. You're surviving on protein bars and the kids' crackers each day. Your ass hasn't been to the gym in so long it's jiggling in places you didn't know *could* jiggle.

And the worst part is that while F.U.N. is on the cards tonight, *you* are not fun anymore. You're not a fun wife or a fun mom. Your nineteen-year-old stepson cannot wait to move out, and you're constantly screaming at your seven- and four-year-olds. You and your husband are basically roommates and you're certainly not having any fun in the bedroom.

But tonight? Tonight is all about that F-word. Tonight is the Network of Executive Women holiday party, and you are going to squeeze every bit of fun out of it that you can.

At 3 p.m. you have a meeting with your vice-president. You do these every year, so you think it's no big deal. You get in early to set up, and your VP rolls in when he's ready.

"Okay, Colleen, add a chart to Slide four. You're sandbagging your sales forecast numbers, increase those. And instead of a five-year history, I want to see ten years. I need all the updates by 8 a.m. tomorrow."

Are you freaking kidding me?

You head back to your office to get to work. By 7 p.m., every light in the office—except yours—is out. There's no way you're making it to that holiday party, and something in you breaks.

I quit. I quit. I can't do this anymore.

But you can't quit. You're the one who pays the mortgage. You're the one who puts food on the table. But you can't keep living like this, either.

So you call your girlfriend Kate, who's a coach. She asks why you can't keep your job, and have the healthy, balanced dynamic you want with your family. And while you would love to have both, you just can't see how it could work.

But Kate can see it, and she works with you for months until you realize that you *can* have it all—when you get clear on what having it all *really* means to you.

One of the first things she has you do is to start meditating. Coming from corporate, you're picturing a bunch of long-haired hippies sitting cross-legged in a grassy field... but you know something has to change, so you heed her advice and start meditating with a very specific question in mind. Your question is simple:

What makes me happy?

Every morning, anywhere from five to ten minutes, for

almost three weeks, you meditate on just that question: what makes you happy? You just ask that question over and over again, and it is crazy what starts coming up.

There are huge things deeply embedded in you that you have never taken the time to think about before. And one core thing stands out above everything else—your passion for helping people, coaching them through their problems so they can create their own answers and solutions.

The next thing Kate helps you see is that you have the control over your situation.

You need to stop blaming your boss for putting you in this job, because you wanted and accepted the position in the first place.

You need to stop blaming your husband, because he gets to work from home and doesn't have to commute like you do.

You need to stop blaming stay-at-home moms for making you feel bad when they take their kids to Disneyland while you're working.

You recognize that everything is your responsibility, and that you made all the choices in that past that have landed you here. And in a single bright moment, you see that you can also make the choices that will change your future.

So as you dive into working on yourself and putting new strategies in place to make the choices you really want at the start of 2014, everything will change for you.

Instead of quitting your job, you will get promoted again. Instead of running your family into the ground, you and your husband will reconnect and you will become a much better mom. Instead of drowning in your work, you will get on top of your new role, *and* start running your own business on the side.

A few years later, you'll quit your corporate job and move full time into helping women just like you to live the 'and' life—to have a powerful career and extraordinary personal life.

You will show them the strategies that help them make that a reality, helping them get clear on what they want, and why. You will help them work out how to align those desires with their vision for their life, and then how to take the small steps, one at a time, to create gradual but constant growth.

So tonight, while you're thinking about the F-word and crying at your desk, remember this: you *can* have a healthy, holistic life. You *can* have it all. You just have to know what having it all really means to you.

I love you.

Colleen.

~

COLLEEN HAUK IS A SPEAKER, TRAINER, CO-AUTHOR OF the bestselling book, *Women Who Ignite*, and creator of YOU SO NEW™, a program designed for successful professionals who fail to take care of their personal life.

Coupled with over fifteen years of corporate leadership and training, Colleen shares her skills, personal experiences and research to empower elite performers in their professional and personal lives. Colleen understands these challenges after suffering her own breaking point where she transformed her circumstances and developed successful methods for a healthy, holistic life. Now she provides her audiences with strategies and resources to 'have it all' without losing it all.

Married to her supportive husband, Matt, they live in Southern California where they were both born and raised. They enjoy life with their beautiful children, Jordan, Ethan, and Reese, camping in the desert, hosting fun-filled evenings with friends, and spending quality time with their nearby extended family.

6

DENISE MILLET

~

You cannot make a life for others if you are not whole and present first.

DEAR DENISE,

I'm writing to you as you were back in 2005, to share some things I have unearthed in the years since then. I think they may be helpful for you to know.

Your twin superpowers of service and observation protected you very well in your turbulent early years; they created quite a fortress to keep the world's tension and anxiety from getting too close.

However, they also fed a natural tendency for you to do too much for others, often at the expense of your true self.

And so you moved into adulthood as a do-er.

You could tackle anything: from coding a complex compiler, landing your dream tech job, moving a household while nine months pregnant, to serving Thanksgiving dinner for twenty-two... nothing was too much for you to handle.

You were on a mission to create a perfect world. You wanted

a world with a fine comfortable home, exciting travels, rich experiences, and all the love and support you could conjure.

You were sure this would guarantee a great life for everyone. You dedicated all of your energy to 'doing it right'. At least, that's what you thought you were doing.

Although you *were* doing an amazing job with the little experience you gleaned from your family of origin, you kept giving away more and more of yourself to keep the machine running. Eventually you were all but invisible in all your service of others.

When you hit that moment, you knew you had to make a choice: your own survival, or keeping the unrealistic dream in place. You had a beautiful 'aha' moment when you came across this passage from *The Bell Jar*, by Sylvia Plath:

> *I saw my life branching out before me like the green fig tree... From the tip of every branch, like a fat purple fig, a wonderful future beckoned and winked... I saw myself sitting in the crotch of this fig tree, starving to death, just because I couldn't make up my mind which of the figs to choose. I wanted each and every one of them, but choosing one meant losing all the rest, and, as I sat there, unable to decide, the figs began to wrinkle and go black, and one by one, they plopped to the ground at my feet.*

No matter what Sylvia Plath meant, the meaning you found in these words—to make a choice or risk losing everything to indecision—gave you the courage to change.

Remember this as you go through the turmoil. Let the words continue to remind you: you are but one person, and you cannot make a life for others if you are not whole and present first.

The dread you will feel knowing you have to choose a path that will upset those you love is natural. You will find your courage and bravely forge ahead, knowing that you *must* or you will not survive. And in the end, the others will also find themselves and will value their own choices all the more.

As the old life fades into the background, I want you to know you will rebuild yourself stronger than ever. You will find your own voice and learn how to use it to share yourself with the world.

By no means will any of it be painless or perfect, but you will find joy and inner peace making decisions and choices true to you, while letting others make theirs.

As Maya Angelou said,

"Do the best you can until you know better. Then when you know better, do better."

With Great Love,
Future You

~

DENISE MILLET HAS BEEN A SYSTEMS CONSULTANT FOR over twenty years; her systems analysis work has honed her ability to evaluate processes, products, and organizations so that actions can bring about needed change.

She writes copy for the technology and consulting industries, specializing in online copy crafted to move readers to action and to produce measurable results for her clients.

Denise is the mother of two amazing adults that inspire her daily. She currently lives in Sea Bright, New Jersey, writing, smelling the salt air, and witnessing the awe of a sunset every day.

To learn more please visit: www.denisemillet.com

NOT-SO-SECRET
LESSON #4

STOP WORRYING ABOUT WHAT OTHER PEOPLE THINK OF YOU

~

The indomitable Eleanor Roosevelt once said, "No one can make you feel inferior without your consent." Or to put it more bluntly, don't let the bastards get you down.

Eleanor was a trailblazer who spoke out in favor of civil rights, labor, and economic reform. Because of this, she made a lot of enemies. The press called her impudent and presumptuous and said it would be a public service if she would simply sit down and shut up.

But Eleanor refused to give in. She was the longest serving First Lady of the United States. During that time, she transformed the role from a hostess in to a social activist. She was the first First Lady to write a daily newspaper column and the first to speak at a national party convention.

Eleanor led the drafting of the Universal Declaration of Human Rights and served as the first U.S. Representative to the United Nations Commission on Human Rights.

She never let other people's opinions stop her, and you shouldn't either. If you find yourself worrying about what other people think, take a moment and listen to these Titanides. Like

Eleanor, each of these women found the courage to tell the rest of the world to go hang and to blaze her own path.

Like Tiara who admonishes her younger self, "Stop bottling up that powerful voice of yours because you're worried about what others think."

Or Pauline who reminds herself to "Never live down to the expectations other have of you... Don't play small to help others feel better about themselves. It never works."

Or Didi who comforts her childhood self, "You are different from the other kids. They can't understand it so they tease you... Remember, you do not have to be like them or liked by them. The only approval you need is your own."

Or Penny who is raised to believe that you must maintain a façade of perfection. Her mother tells her she must keep an impeccably clean house, wear the best clothes, and care deeply about what others think of her. Until one day Penny finally stops listening to her mother's voice and starts listening to her own.

Or Melinda, who, after years of hard times, comforts her younger self saying, "One day, you'll no longer care what people think of you. You'll finally understand that the ones you need to impress, already love you as you are."

So take a lesson from Eleanor Roosevelt and blaze your own trail. The only opinion about your life that matters is your own.

❧ I ❧

PAULINE LONGDON

~

Don't play small to help others feel better about themselves. It never works.

HEY YOUNGER PAULINE,

How's life treating you? No need to answer that, I already know. I've been watching you for a while, and now I know you better than you know yourself. I've shared all your highs and lows, and your so-called mistakes, along the way.

I was with you in September in 2005, when you reached your lowest moment and wanted to end it all. I was with you as you sped towards that tree, and I breathed a heavy sigh of relief as you changed your mind at the last minute. And I was with you as you struggled to make sense of life for a long time afterwards.

You had always been such a prolific reader, so to see you without a book in your hand for so long was torture. But it was even worse watching you only use pencils to write, because you didn't believe you were worth the ink. I saw how hard it was for you to retrain your mind to read and write again. But you did it, and slowly you climbed your way out of depression's darkness.

In time you will learn never to live down to the expectations others have of you. People you trusted set the bar way too low for you, and many wrote you off. They said you'd never amount to much, but they were so wrong.

They told you that you'd never be a good copywriter because you're female... and through sheer grit, pig-headed determination and countless hours of hard work, you will make them eat their ugly words.

But there was a slight truth in those ugly words. The fact is that you'll never be a good copywriter because you're female— you're an *exceptional* copywriter, because you're *you*. You will become quite the wordsmith, and you will need no qualifiers to define you.

You get to set your own bar, so hold your head high.

I know it hurt you when the people you looked up to most wouldn't accept you. Because you only wanted to be friends... but just know, it wasn't you. It was them, and it was immature and stupid. Some people just don't like having friends who make them feel bad about themselves.

You don't do it intentionally, but when people work hard for what they have, they resent others who seem to get things easily or have a natural talent (they choose not to see how hard you work, so they'll have a reason to reject you). I wish I could tell you not to waste your time trying to fit in, when you are clearly made to stand out. But your kind heart makes you want to help people, often at your own expense; don't worry—eventually, you'll stop doing that.

So go out and find your real tribe—the people who get you and really appreciate you. The people who lift you up and never tear you down. There are many like you, and when you get out of your comfort zone you will find them. You don't have to go it alone, and it's better if you don't.

Pauline, you have a remarkable insight into humanity. Sometimes you feel that you see too much, but it's a precious gift. Don't let others make you second-guess yourself—you're usually right—and if there's one piece of loving advice I can give you, it's this:

Don't play small to help others feel better about themselves. It never works.

Remember that on that dark day back in 2005, you made a decision to stay here. And I'm glad you did, because you have a big future ahead of you. You're here to make a difference, and there's no time left for playing small. You've got this.

You have gone from not being able to read or write, to being a best-selling author and being paid to write. You have come so far and you still have so far to go. Let's do this!

Love Pauline, (your #1 fan.)

P.S. You can stop dyeing your hair. It's time for you to get the 'Longdon Look'—you totally rock the gray!

PAULINE LONGDON IS A BESTSELLING AUTHOR, RETIRED Army Major, and Copywriting/Marketing Strategist. She specializes in writing to the conscious consumer and has written for over forty-seven different industries and sub-industries.

Pauline enjoys translating her clients' heartfelt and mindful messages into marketing assets. Her background as a Registered Nurse and growing up in the "Land Down Under" has given Pauline a unique perspective on life and a wicked sense of humor. When she's not writing, she's busy making stunning jewelry, being a podcaster, mentoring copywriters and learning new skills. She has an insatiable curiosity and an adventurous soul.

You can find out more about Pauline at www.TheCopyAlchemist.com or www.FromDepressions-Darkness.com

❧ 2 ❧

TIARA COLE

～

You knew that—no matter what happened—you would work it out along the way. And you did.

Dear Tiara,

If only you knew the places you'll go, the people you'll meet, the adventures you'll have—it will take you a while to realize it, but it's going to be one heck of an amazing life, girl!

You're great with people, a truly caring soul. Nine times out of ten, you're the life of the party... but inside you often don't feel that way. Even though you've built a business and a life you love, there are still days when you lack the confidence to speak up for yourself, when you feel hurt, angry, sad, ugly, or scared.

You bottle up that powerful voice of yours because you care too much about what others think. You back down from fights because you're convinced in your own mind there's no way you can win. You need to learn to attack problems head on, so you can stop defeating yourself before you even try to make a stand, argue a point or share an idea.

Any time you start having those ugly, nasty feelings, think

back to yourself at nineteen. Think of that day on the bus, rolling through Ecuador towards Peru, while you were volunteering your way around South America.

You were so confident, you said yes to everything, you knew that—no matter what happened—you would work it out along the way. And you did. Trust in that.

Remember that she is still in you, Tiara Cole, and that you are powerful.

Start listening to your personal support group of family and friends that see, plain as day, that you are meant to be a rockstar.

Believe them when they say you're beautiful, smart, talented, strong, desirable, and that you're going to make a name for yourself.

Believe them when they say you can do anything you set your mind to. Remember, they love you and see the bigger picture when you can't. So learn to trust those who have a clearer vision than you. They are guiding you towards amazing things, and a life where your work fully supports your true passion for volunteering and helping people.

Appreciate the experience of others to help you overcome the obstacles you will face. Take those experiences and build a stronger foundation, using their strengths to overcome your weaknesses.

Lastly, and this is the most important thing—know that I'm proud of you. You still want to hear it from others, but if *I'm* proud of you, that's really all that matters. You're going to face challenges, experience hurts and suffer disappointments, but you have the strength to endure whatever comes your way.

So, for the record, I am incredibly proud of you. Never forget you are a precious gem, and here's to an amazing future.

Your #1 fan,

Tiara

～

TIARA COLE IS A DIRECT RESPONSE COPYWRITER FOR THE alternative health niche. As a teen she saw how much freedom copywriting offered, and started her own freelance copywriting and graphic design company called Crown Ink Designs.

What Tiara enjoys most about being a copywriter is the freedom to travel the world... spend as much time as she wants with her four incredible nephews... and dedicate seventy hours a month to her Bible educational work.

www.crowninkdesigns.com

❊ 3 ❊

DIDI KING

~

You are meant to carve a new path where others will follow you.

DEAR DIDI,

You are a beautiful, powerful, creative being. This may be hard for you to grasp with what you are going through, but trust me on this one.

Your parents love you and did the best they could with their limited beliefs. Don't blame them for your struggles.

You are different from the other kids. They can't understand it so they tease you. They try to bring you down to their level. Their ignorance causes them to do it; it has nothing to do with you.

Society's conditioning of the masses calls to you to conform... to be like them... to be *liked* by them. Resist! In the grand scheme of things, the only approval you need is yours.

As much as you believe these interactions to be devastating, they are, in fact, the constant building blocks of your indestructible spirit.

Every time someone wipes their feet on you, you gain

perspective. Every blow to your self-respect sparks your desire to become more. Every tear you shed serves to flush out the poison of opinion.

Every disparaging word or action toward you in their attempts to break you down only result in a strength that is undeniable.

Embrace these moments. Give gratitude to the Universe for placing you on your path. Send love to everyone who hurt you, because they did you a favor. Forgive, forgive, forgive. All is well.

There is no one to blame. No one holding you back. As soon as you fully internalize this truth the world will need to watch out!

You will become a beacon for so many searching for their true selves. Your experiences will allow you to illuminate their paths. You can help them shed the weight of ignorance and stagnation. You never give up, and so abundance and success are yours.

What you don't know yet is that your isolation will help you understand your truth. You weren't meant to follow the crowd. You are meant to carve a new path where others will follow you.

You will learn this wonderful truth when you begin to question your situation... when you realize there is more for you and you being your search.

This search will take you on a winding path. There will be some obstacles in the road. Don't go around them, stop and appreciate the lesson each one brings. You'll find it, and with it your growth to who you are today.

You will find some awesome mentors to help guide you. Soak up everything they teach you. Their wisdom is priceless. All you learn from them will help you become the awesome mentor, guide, and coach you are today.

People don't get you yet, but they will.

You are an old soul.

You are a beautiful intuitive being.

You see the good in everyone.

And remember this... the good you see in others is a reflection of the good that exists in you. Digest that for a moment. And when people tell you that you're awesome... believe them!

Everything you need is inside of you already just waiting for you to open the door. Self-image is what you choose to believe, not what someone forced upon you as an innocent child.

Perseverance is your shield, empathy is your strength, intuition is your guiding principle.

Don't you dare let anyone break you. You choose who you are. You choose your power. You choose your path. You choose to be the true Titanide you are!

I want you to know all of this, but I'm not sending this letter to you...

Your life is so full of abundance right now. You have a wonderful husband who loves each of your perfect imperfections. You have three beautiful children who bring you more joy than you can perceive possible. You have found your calling... coaching others to find their internal power. You appreciate all you have, and give of yourself freely because of every joy and sorrow you've gone through.

If I send you this letter, dearest Didi, you will carve a different path. Now that I see where I've come from, I can't take any of it away from you.

With Love,
Didi

~

DIDI KING, OWNER OF KING QUANTUM THOUGHT, IS A Certified Thinking Into Results Consultant who works with her clients to create the lifestyle and business they want.

Didi enjoys interacting with individuals, groups and companies to help them discover their deepest goals and desires. She is a perpetual student of human growth and potential. Didi is thrilled to be able to share her passion and guide people to live happier, healthier, more abundant lives.

Didi has been an entrepreneur in publishing, both music and print, for over twenty years. She is a recognized music engraving expert and has won a great number of MPA Paul Revere Awards for Graphic Excellence. She has worked as both a fitness coach and instructor helping people realize the importance of mindset in achieving their fitness goals.

The power of thought and the Law of Attraction are undeniable forces in reaching your highest potential. Didi is passionate about teaching people how to move past the paradigms that are holding them back. Learn more at www. kingquantumthought.com

❧ 4 ❧

MELINDA MINETTE

∼

Even though you're a princess, you're no longer a damsel in distress.

DEAR MELINDA,

I am writing this letter to you at a crossroads in your life. I'm sorry to tell you this, but, you're getting divorced. Some days you will feel like you're being crushed.

You'll make mistakes that will ruin your life as you currently know it, distance you from those you love most, and nearly make you lose your mind.

I wish I could tell you something that could make you avoid those mistakes. But I can't, and they will stay with you for the rest of your life.

But what I can say is this:

You'll live through this. It will feel unbearable... but it will pass.

You'll mend most of the hearts that were broken, including yours.

You'll feel relieved, eventually, and find freedom, peace of mind, and calmness of heart.

You'll become different. In ways both good and bad. You won't allow abusive people into your life any longer. You'll know real hunger, poverty, and pain.

But you'll come out on the other side of the darkness with valuable traits.

You know that hard times will come, but they only stay hard when you stop moving. So you will keep pushing forward.

You'll no longer care what people think of you. The ones you need to impress love you as you are.

You'll see that even though you're a princess, you're no longer a damsel in distress.

You'll learn how important it is to work on how you feel rather than how you look. You'll learn to love hard work, and the results that work brings you.

You'll learn life's most valuable things don't have a price tag. And no one can take them from you.

Melinda, you will learn what you should've learned long ago: happiness comes from within. You can't buy it, borrow it, or get it from someone else. It grows inside you in proportion to the amount of yourself you give to others.

Don't fear being alone. Or growing old, or singing your own tune, or dancing to a different rhythm.

Don't look back to your twenties and think about how pretty you used to be. Every decade has its own beauty. You're starting to experience your best years. It's hard to believe with all the tears. But it's true. Remember looking at Mom's photos in her forties and fifties? She said she was most beautiful then... learn from the scars you don't earn.

See yourself, at this moment, as the most beautiful you'll be. Those years, from forty-two through forty-five, will chisel you into the person you should be. As you go through it, trust this time to sculpt you into a unique piece of art.

The adventure is beginning. The good part of your life starts now!

I love you, little moo.

MELINDA MINETTE CHOSE TO BE A COPYWRITER IN THE natural health and lifestyle field because she lives the healthy lifestyle she learns. Her copywriting services empower people to take control of their health. And she believes everyone should have a long and happy life, full of memories.

❧ 5 ❧

PENNY HUNT

❦

What you think is the only thing that matters.

MY DEAR PENNY,

So, here you are. Thirty-two. My goodness... for all you've been through already, one would think you would be finished struggling.

And yet you are.

You fell in love at a young age... no one saw that coming, but you knew it was the right thing for you. When Ken proposed, you fought your parents and made the case for your marriage to him at nineteen years old.

Your Mom was *so* against it, and your Dad wasn't thrilled either. Although, according to him, no one would have been good enough.

However, instead of suffering the humiliation of having you elope—what would people think?—they caved, in part due to your persuasive ability, and supported the 'perfect' December wedding.

You moved to Huntsville, Alabama, and set about

housekeeping while he served out his last stretch in the Army. It was a dream come true... and then came your first big disaster.

After four short months together, you were shocked and heartbroken by the orders deploying him to Korea for a thirteen-month tour.

Left behind, crushed, you went back to Pennsylvania to share a house with your sister. You counted the days until Ken's return, robbed of your honeymoon year by his service to the country.

I'm so proud of how you handled this. You were so stoic.

You kept telling people, *"At least he's not in Vietnam!"* You put on a big smile and a positive attitude, and you got through it. Your highschool 'Problems of Democracy' teacher, Mr. Moody, had taught you above all else to 'be flexible', and at this point in your life you took that lesson fully to heart.

Once Ken returned, you recommitted to each other, and learned to fall in love all over again to continue your marriage. Many would have chosen to let it drift away and divorced. But then again... what would people think?

After a few rocky years of financial troubles and job adjustments, you were in love and finally back on track. So much so that you decided to start your family.

The pregnancy did not go well and at twenty-eight weeks, you both took another gut-wrenching blow. You went into premature labor and Ken delivered your baby girl on the front porch of your home.

It was beyond what any parent should have to bear.

With today's medicines, she might have made it. But, in 1974, she was just too little. You both suffered her death three days later, and the funeral a week after her birth. You will feel that loss in the depths of your heart every day for the rest of your life.

You wanted to sue the hospital, and the doctors... but what would people think? All the money in the world would not bring her back, but you wanted the doctors to pay, to have someone to blame.

But life went on, and it brought you the joy of two healthy children—Kevin in 1975 and Sara in 1978.

You did the best you could, with what you had, and being a good loving mom was the focal point of your existence. Despite the dull dishtowels your mother always criticized you for, you were happy.

And yes, Ken's career made you move thirteen times, but you made it an adventure each time and survived. After all... this is what 'being flexible' was all about.

Even so, you struggled to maintain a façade of perfection. You had been raised to care, deeply, about what other people thought of you. Your mother could not bear the thought of other people thinking badly of her or her family, and you absorbed this anxiety.

But finally, one strange day, you will discover that you can stop carrying your mother's worries.

Your parents will finally come to visit you in California. You and Ken will plan a nice visit taking them to places in San Francisco they would never see otherwise. But your mom will ruin it.

She will immediately start in on you about how hurtful it is for her to have us so far away. How could we do this to her? It's so painful that she pretends her grandkids are dead—she just can't bear explaining to people that they are so far away. She will go on and on, and then end with the backhanded suggestion that if you ever wanted to leave Ken, you and the kids would always be welcome to come home.

You will be stunned. Confused. Hurt. Furious. How could your mom—who had always seemed so perfect—say such wrong, horrible things?

And then it will hit you. She was not perfect at all. She kept an impeccably clean house. She kept us in the best clothes. But her motives were more driven by what people would think than anything else.

And at what cost? She stressed about every little detail. It consumed much time she could have been having fun and doing things with us instead of fussing if we looked good doing it.

You realize at that moment that she was not perfect, and you will also realize that you are not perfect—nor do you need to be.

What will other people think? You will instantly see that it doesn't matter, and that you don't need to care about it anymore. What *you* think is the only thing that matters.

Shedding that burden will free you from living a life of stress and unhappiness, and will allow you to become a woman whose life is about others—helping, taking care of people, enjoying and loving life.

So I say to you, and to my sisters in this life:

1. Always be flexible. If something doesn't go the way you planned, know that if you are flexible, it will all fall into place eventually.

2. You are not perfect, and more importantly, you don't have to be perfect.

With love to you all from my life,

Penny Hunt

PENNY HUNT BEGAN HER WRITING CAREER AS A PART-TIME fun thing to do back in 2009. Writing for a variety of industries and clients, she became more serious about her writing after she retired in 2015. She aspired to add more clients and money to help with retirement and extras.

Due to some changing circumstances and again being flexible, an opportunity presented itself for her to become the owner of her business Penny Hunt Copywriting LLC.

She is an AWAI COS and PWA member and also is an AWAI COS Mentor and serves on the AWAI Reviewer Team.

NOT-SO-SECRET
LESSON #5

LEAP BEFORE YOU'RE READY

~

Study after study shows that women take less risks than men. Some blame biology or evolution or economics. But the bottom line is, female entrepreneurs tend to be more risk-averse. We're the remember your seat belt, cross your T's dot your I's, and alway-floss-your-teeth kind of gals.

Not only that, but the more stressed we are, the less risk we take. And that's bad news for women—because most entrepreneurs are neck deep in stress, most of the time. So while we're waiting until we're a hundred percent prepared for every possible scenario before we take a risk, men are taking the leap ahead of us.

The women in this chapter were scared, they didn't feel ready, but they took the leap anyway. Erin, co-founder of 4Patriots, one of the fastest growing private companies in America, reminds her younger self, "You only ever have to take the steps that's right in front of you. So don't invest every single step with so much significance."

Laurie, a sports writer, flings herself into the unknown over and over again. She reminds her younger self, "Were you ready to make the leap? No. But when you finally stop dwelling in your fears, you'll find it was the best move to make."

Michele spent thirty-five years in direct marketing and creative management for a large New York publisher. When she finally makes the leap at age fifty-five to start her own business, she too tells her younger self, "When you finally take the plunge to strike out on your own, you'll be the happiest you've ever been, and you'll wish you had done it sooner."

When Nicole loses both her career and her husband in twenty-four hours, she is forced to take a leap. She tells her younger self, "If you wait until you can see far enough along the path to feel comfortable, you will stay stuck where you are... and you'll never know what you're truly capable of."

When Diane takes a leap and mails a letter on her thirtieth birthday, she has no idea that letter will set off a chain of events that changes everything.

Many of the Titanides in this chapter were filled with doubt, but as Patricia tells her younger self, "If I could remove the doubt, I would. But it's part of the journey and part of the price of leaping towards something new and scary." Feel the doubt and take the leap anyway.

You might not feel ready in this moment, but you're never going to be a hundred percent ready. There is never going to be a perfect time to start your business or ask for that promotion or launch a new product. So stop waiting and leap already. Chances are, you'll wish you'd done it sooner.

ERIN BALER

~

You only ever have to take the next step.

DEAR ERIN,

If there's one thing you should know, it's that you only ever have to take the step that's right in front of you.

I know you were scared about moving to Nashville.

A lot of people thought you and your husband were *crazy* for giving up the security of two six-figure corporate jobs, selling your nice house and letting go of your baby's spot in daycare. They love you, and they were concerned for you; they just could not understand you. But you knew there is more to life than going to the same job every day and leaving your little girl in daycare for fifty hours a week.

I know you were scared about joining your husband to work on the business he started at your kitchen table.

You worked at the same company for ten years after you graduated, and then you were scared that you might not be good at anything else. You tortured yourself with this fear and self-doubt, wondering if you would ever be able to do something else.

Moving to Nashville forced the issue, and you started to realize that just because you don't know what the end of the journey looks like doesn't mean you can't take the next step.

I know you were scared about hiring people.

You never felt that betting on you and your husband was a risk—you didn't mind betting your family's livelihood on yourselves, because you trust each other and knew what you both were good at, but asking other people to put their livelihoods in your hands felt incredibly risky.

But you know now that when you take the leap, when you just step into what's in front of you, it always works out.

You know now that Nashville was the right place for you.

You were lucky to have been able to sell your house in Connecticut and have some savings when you moved there. The move was easy and it gave you the time with your daughter that you wanted so much. Your parents were thrilled that you were back in Tennessee—their home in Memphis was now much closer—and you got to have a business that fit your lifestyle and gave you control over your livelihood.

You know now that you and your husband were right to be confident in each other.

You still think he's the best person in the world, and everything you do together works out. Building your company together allowed you to play well off each other. His confidence and his ability to lead has driven you forward, and your ability to implement and follow through every day keeps the progress coming. He has always been more of a risk taker than you, he's always been the visionary, and you've always been the executor. You both know that neither of you would do anything that would put your family or business in any kind of danger, so while he wants it to go fast and you want it to go safe, together you make it go right.

You know now that hiring people will be the best decision you could have made for your business.

You realized that you couldn't do the things you wanted to in order to make the business better and stronger—the things you *knew* needed to happen—if you didn't get over yourselves. You realized that there were people out there who would be excited to do this with you, and were happy to be a part of your company. It was kind of a mind-blowing thing, that people thought it was really cool, even if you didn't feel like you knew what you were doing. The company has grown to seventy-five people (and counting), with multiple product lines, and it continues to be more and more fun. It's not how you had envisioned it at the start, but it gets better every day. It has all been worth it.

And Erin, know that some days you will still be scared.

But you only ever have to take the next step. You just have to do the next thing that makes sense, and then the next thing, and as long as you're continuing to learn and grow and you want to keep getting better, those opportunities will keep presenting themselves.

And if something doesn't work out, you haven't ruined all decisions ever for the rest of your life—you just tried one thing that didn't work, and at the very least you will learn something from it.

So don't invest every single step with so much significance. Just do the thing. No one is going to do it for you, and no one is going to come give you permission. Ideas do not spring fully formed from the ether for you to just run with—you have to bring them to life yourself, because you're never going to get some blessing from on high that makes you feel a hundred percent okay.

If you want your life to be different, you have to do it for yourself. You don't need to know where the journey is going to end. You don't need to know what all the steps look like. You just have to decide, and take the step that's right in front of you.

Love,

Erin

~

ERIN BALER IS THE CO-FOUNDER OF 4PATRIOTS, LLC, A direct-to-consumer e-commerce company that helps Americans become more independent and self-reliant.

After spending nearly a decade learning marketing in the corporate world, Erin and her husband Allen moved from the Northeast to Nashville, Tennessee where they founded 4Patriots, with the goal of creating a company that delivers great products at a great value, treats every customer like they would want to be treated, and is a great place for great people to work.

Since its founding, the business has grown from a two-person, kitchen table startup to a company that employs over seventy people in multiple states. The company was included on the Inc. 5000 list of fastest-growing private companies in America in 2013.

Erin thrives on capturing ideas, creating plans to make them a reality and driving execution. Her mission is to pull together all the different functions in the organization and get the whole team marching down the path to make the 4Patriots vision happen.

She enjoys identifying and solving business problems, bottlenecks and roadblocks, as well as creating and retaining a high-performing team that is aligned with the company's Core Values.

Erin holds a B.A. in Communications from the University Of Pennsylvania. She lives in Nashville with her husband and three daughters.

LAURIE GARRISON

*It's not what they think of you;
it's what you think of yourself.*

Dear Laurie,

The road ahead is going to be full of challenges. Some will be big, some will be small, but none you can't handle. I wish I could say something to make it easier, but I can't—you just have to go through it.

There will be times you'll wish things were different. You'll regret some actions you'll take and some of the words you'll say. But all you can do is learn and grow, and keep learning and keep growing. Because every action and every step brings you closer to who you are now.

And the woman you are now is finally out on her own, working the freelance life full-time. Were you ready to make the leap? No. But when you finally get out of your head, when you finally stopped dwelling on your fears, when you finally quit building obstacles in your own way, you'll find it was the best move to make. You'll wish you had done it sooner.

Don't be stunned when you're told you take conservative steps—all of those slow, steady, deliberate actions lead to massive leaps forward. Three times in your life, you'll quit your job without having another one lined up and, at the same time, uproot your life and move to another city. Each time you do, you'll launch yourself further ahead on your path.

And those same people who lauded you for being so deliberate will be amazed at your audacity in flinging yourself into the unknown (and maybe a little jealous when it works so well for you).

But in the end, it's not what they think of you; it's what you think of yourself. And when you finally realize and accept that, this is when you'll really start to flourish.

But I can't write a letter to you, my younger self, without imparting the one piece of advice I received in my forties that I wish I had learned in my twenties. Two simple words that will turn your life around: Just Breathe. When you start to get angry, just breathe and you'll find the issue isn't worth that emotion. When fear starts to creep in, just breathe and you'll see how unfounded it is. And when joy and happiness find you, just breathe and savor the feelings and moments.

You have an interesting journey ahead. And just like the roller coasters you love to ride, it will be full of ups and downs. So ride the highs and weather the lows and, like the roller coaster, trust that you'll come out in the right place on the other side.

It's your journey to own. And you wouldn't have it any other way.

From your future self,
Laurie

~

LAURIE GARRISON SPECIALIZES IN WRITING BUSINESS awards entries. She also writes sales copy and marketing content, primarily for companies in the sports industry. In 2017, she left the corporate world to move into freelance writing.

Laurie spent more than thirty years in the sports industry as a writer, magazine editor, copy editor, convention and luncheon planner and running awards program. She has turned her expertise in running awards programs into a writing specialty and now, as her featured service offering, works with her clients on consulting and writing their awards entries. More than seventy-five percent of the entries Laurie has written have won or been chosen as finalists, a mark well above the industry average.

Learn more about Laurie at www.LaurieGarrison.com

❧ 3 ❧

PATRICIA MOYER

∾

Be audacious enough to believe in you.

DEAR INTREPID PATRICIA,

I'm reaching out to you on this day in 1987 to let you know that no matter what happens—even thirty years from now—your life, like today, will continue to be exciting and so full of promise.

Today, you are conquering the old boys club of filmmaking and winning accolades and awards. At twenty-seven, you have a corner office with the big window and the inevitable ficus tree. Your work is creative, exciting, and exhausting. You've married that great guy, Mark, who at first underestimated you. You've even learned to fly a plane.

But, life has a way of progressing and moving in directions we simply cannot see. It'll happen to you in a big way, and you'll learn to leap, over and over again.

You'll make your first big, scary decision ten years from now. It's a decision that, right now, you are absolutely dead-set against, and it will change you, humble you, and give you great joy.

This new adventure—that of raising and homeschooling four wonderful kids—will be one of the strangest, hardest, and most rewarding times of your life.

Now, I realize that I've probably made you very uncomfortable with this knowledge—you only want one kid, I know. But, your first love is teaching, so let that knowledge dull the shock.

And, here's another eye-opener—you will, for the next twenty years, be riddled with a thing you know little of today— doubt. Doubt of the job you're doing (there's no accolades, raises, or performance reviews for moms). Doubt that it will have been worth giving up the dream career. Doubt in yourself.

If I could remove the doubt, I would. But it's part of the journey and part of the price of leaping towards something new and scary.

And I'm not through. You'll do something even scarier and more uncomfortable, and here's where my advice comes in.

Once you know your kids are doing well and moving on... you need to do the same. You need to take another leap.

You'll turn to the thing that always worked for you: writing. But instead of it supporting your career and your teaching, it will be your life's work and new exciting purpose.

You'll call yourself a writer for the first time.

And because you'll do this on your own, you'll come to know fear. Fear of being out of the working world for too long. Fear of this thing called the Internet that roared to life while you taught Greek Mythology and Algebra. Fear that your skills are gone, you are obsolete, and you have nothing to offer this new and strange world.

So, here's my advice:

Be fearless when you want to dive under the covers and hide.

Be bold when those who would hire you are half your age (or worse, your son's age).

Be brave when you feel like a fraud.

And, most important: be audacious enough to believe in you.

The feelings you have today that tell you that you can conquer anything you take on, use them, at age fifty-seven, to be brave enough to prosper or fail, even in front of your kids who never stop learning by your example.

It will be the greatest lesson you could give them, and the greatest gift to yourself.

I believe in you. Go get 'em.

Patricia

PATRICIA MOYER HAS OVER THIRTY YEARS OF EXPERIENCE writing across numerous industries and causes. Her career started as a script writer and producer in cable television access which led to numerous awards including a Cable ACE for documentary film production and a coveted Emmy nomination. Today, she has turned her love of writing into a successful business that allows her the freedom to work from home.

For fun, she also enjoys challenging and mentoring high school juniors and seniors as they struggle to write their college essays. And she knows what she's doing—three of her four children have successfully been accepted and graduated college. Her fourth is next, but at thirteen years old, she still has some time to write that entrance essay.

For more information:

PATRICIA@MOYERCONSULTANTGROUP.COM

WWW.LINKEDIN.COM/IN/PATRICIAMOYERCOPY/

❧ 4 ❧

MICHELE WOLK

❧

Trusting in your abilities and relying on your gut is the key to fulfillment and happiness.

DEAR MICHELE,

Who would have thought that a bright-eyed college graduate with a degree in politics and economics would have wound up in the circulation department of a major magazine publisher in New York?

You didn't even know what 'circulation marketing' was, but it was in the Big Apple, and that's all that mattered to you. That entry-level job was the launchpad of a thirty-five-year career in direct marketing and creative management for publishers, supplement companies, and associations.

You learned early on that it would be necessary to change positions frequently in order to move up the ladder and to gain new experiences, especially in smaller companies where there was no real growth potential.

You learned to go to as many industry events as possible, in order to learn and to make important career-building contacts. It became clear that it would be crucial to do your very best and retain the highest ethical standards in all work relationships, since the direct marketing industry is small, and great contacts open doors.

You learned that it is important to surround yourself with smart, forward-thinking coworkers and to try to stay positive, even in difficult situations.

In hindsight, there are things you could have done differently.

You didn't need to invest so many weekends and nights responding to emails and perfecting your work, and you could have taken more time off when raising your infant twins, instead of burning the candle at both ends.

You could have let go of the *"what will they do without me"* attitude, and let conflict roll off your back more.

Maybe you could have realized that no job is forever, and when things changed suddenly, you could have looked for the writing on the wall before things really started to deteriorate. You should have listened to your peers when they told you that you were good enough to work for yourself.

And while all those lessons were tough, you learned that trusting in your abilities and relying on your gut is the key to fulfillment and happiness. Everything you went through prepared you for the day, at age fifty-five, that you decided it was time to "hang out a shingle" and start something of your own.

It will be scary—even with your experience and contacts—to take the leap, and to trust in your worth enough to call yourself a consultant. You will have some failures, but every experience just makes you better. Don't expect everything to be smooth, but keep the faith. Know who you are, know your value, and keep pushing forward past the bumps in the road.

All in all, you've been pretty lucky and fulfilled. Having taken the plunge to strike out on your own, you'll be the happiest you've ever been, and you'll wish you had done it sooner.

Love,

Michele

~

MICHELE WOLK IS THE PROUD MOM OF ADULT TWIN daughters and is married to Artie.

She has been working in the direct marketing industry for over thirty years in various publishing and marketing organizations and was most recently the Creative Director at Bottom Line Publications. She is now self-employed and owner of Michele Wolk Marketing. When not working, she spends her time taking long walks with her cockapoo Bailey, biking, reading and watching the latest Netflix production.

5

NICOLE PIPER

~

One step is all you need to move forward.

DEAR LITTLE GIRL,

You're ten! And what a tenacious girl you are! This trait will serve you well in the years ahead. So will your resilience and passion for life.

Your love of horses is as strong as ever. And you're very creative, too. You love to express your creativity every way you can—through art, writing, music, drama, and even ballet. This is a special time in your life... enjoy it. And enjoy this time with your family, too.

Because things will change. And I'm sorry to tell you this... but some of the changes ahead will be very difficult. In fact, your life will be shattered beyond recognition.

Your teen years are just ahead, and they will be hard. Not too long from now, you'll start to lose many of the things you love. Some things you'll feel you have to give up, like ballet, and others will be taken from you, like horseback riding. And eventually, the family life you love will be pulled apart by disease.

You'll feel a growing gap that separates you from the person you were when you were little. You'll be driven to find your place in the world. That drive is what sparks the start of your amazing journey.

And if I told you where this journey will take you, you wouldn't believe me.

You'll live in France and Kenya... then your profession will take you around the globe... and eventually you'll have a family of your own.

And then once again, the life you know will be taken away from you. First, your thirteen-year marriage will end, and twenty-four hours later, the career you've had for twenty-nine years will be taken from you too.

As everything goes to pieces, you'll expect a full-blown panic attack to hit.

But it doesn't.

And in a moment of clarity, the dream you have secretly nourished—the writer's life!—will rise up out of the mess. The copywriting program you once purchased is waiting in your study, and somewhere in yourself you know that what's coming next is going to be *good*.

You don't know where copywriting is going to take you (and I'm not going to tell you all the details) but you'll decide to give it your very best shot for two years.

In fact, your decision to simply *expect* it to work seems to put you in the right place at the right time, over and over again. You'll get personal guidance from some of the best in the business, and soon enough you'll have more work than you can handle. It's going to be extraordinary!

But at this moment, while you're young, there are three important things for you to know. They will help you in the days and years ahead.

First, pay attention to your intuition and how you feel energetically. Know that what you think about expands. Protect yourself from negativity (especially negative people), and don't waste an ounce of your magnificent brain power on negative thoughts. Learn to meditate as soon as you can; it is the key to everything you will need in the days ahead.

Second, understand that comfort zones can also be prisons. You need to embrace challenges that push you beyond where you are now, and try to accept that trials will also play an important role for you. They may come about in a way that seems unfair, but even the most difficult trials can be sources of astounding growth if you let them.

And this brings me to perhaps the most important of the three:

Don't stay stuck waiting until you see a clear path ahead of you. The fact is, that path will rarely emerge. And even if you think you can see where a path leads, it's most likely an illusion. If you wait until you can see far enough along the path to feel comfortable, you will stay stuck where you are... and you'll never know what you're truly capable of.

This is most important to remember during difficult times, when a dense fog keeps you from seeing even two steps ahead. Remember, one step is all you need to move forward. And when you take it, you'll be able to see the next one more clearly. Expect it, and it will happen.

Now off you go, little girl... you have an amazing life ahead of you!

xo

Nicole

∾

NICOLE PIPER IS A GLOBAL BRAND STRATEGIST AND loyalty marketer turned direct response copywriter. Prior to opening the doors of Piper Marketing Solutions, Nicole built multi-million dollar businesses around the globe for well-known brands such as MTV, The Sharper Image, and Pokémon. She also led the launch of Nickelodeon's licensed consumer products business in over thirty countries.

Now a direct response copywriter and marketer, Nicole combines her writing skills and brand development expertise into a unique approach she calls "direct response branding." This approach helps companies build a powerful connection with their core customer, build their business, and build their brand.

Nicole is the proud mother of a son, Alexander. When she's not writing, Nicole likes to spend her time outdoors or in the kitchen cooking up delicious meals to share with family and friends.

CONNECT WITH NICOLE ON LINKEDIN:
   www.linkedin.com/in/nicolekpiper/

OR THROUGH HER WEBSITE:
   www.pipermarketingsolutions.com

6

DIANE SWEENEY

~

If we know ourselves, we're always home, anywhere.

HEY THERE LOVE,

The letter you are holding in your hand—the one you wrote today on your thirtieth birthday—will change everything. As soon as it is opened, actions will be taken that set the course for the rest of your life.

You've reached deep inside to know yourself these last two years since quitting your corporate job—spent time with family, friends and strangers, worked at odd jobs. You tried to 'find yourself' living in the Hamptons in the summers, but you found that the creative beach writer's life wasn't quite what you wanted either.

Through this all you've remained sure about one thing: you aren't going to let life change you... you will change life.

You've experienced new jobs, new places, new and broken relationships. You may have wavered at some points—and lost respect for yourself—but that isn't going to happen again. You are wiser, but still unsure of what 'home' is going to be for you.

But you've got a hunch... and you hunger to find that place in your heart to call home.

So when you send that letter, you will risk embarrassment and a piece of your heart. But you will not lose your sense of self-worth ever again.

There will be a tsunami of changes, and at times, self-doubt and wonder.

The guy who receives your letter will respond, you will reconnect, and in six months you will marry. You will move to Pennsylvania, stepping out of your New York world of spiked heels, big hair, and padded shoulder jackets to live on three acres in the woods.

Soon, your very pregnant self will sit in a cold, aluminum folding chair, in a shell of a house, reading the book *How to Build a House* to your husband as he hangs drywall.

You will sit on the sofa with your firstborn as he breastfeeds, cursing the desolation of the woods, the distance between you and your family, believing you don't have friends or a life.

You will drive miles and miles on the New Jersey Turnpike as you work hard to maintain relationships with friends and family in New York.

You will dive deeper into mother love with the birth of your second son, and deep into despair after the stillborn birth of a third.

To bring in extra money—and to have kids for your kids to play with (after all, you live in the woods!), you will run a daycare from your home for nine years. You will sell Avon products. You will immerse yourself in a nutrition business. You will head committee after committee at school, Little League, Scouts, church and women's groups.

You will learn how to follow the road out of woods into the homes of new friends. Some friendships become strong, forever relationships. Some run their course. Each is valued for their wisdom and worth they bring to your life.

You will write newsletters for your volunteer groups. You will be blogging before it becomes a 'thing.' You will learn how to become an online marketer and copywriter. You will create a work style, lifestyle and freelance business that will bring you peace of heart and happiness.

Your marriage will be tested year after year. Lack of money, your husband's constant threat of lay-off, property that needs constant attention, miscarriages and stillbirths, and all the trials life brings.

But not once will you and he ever lose respect for one another or love for the life you have created together.

Not once do you ever wonder what would have happened if you had not quit that job or put the letter in the mailbox.

Warmth, love and respect will be abundant in the home and life you and Don build together.

You changed life. And life changed you. You found your Home.

Remember what Glinda the Good Witch says in *The Wonderful Wizard of Oz*: "Home is a place we all must find, child. It's not just a place where you eat or sleep. Home is knowing. Knowing your mind, knowing your heart, knowing your courage. If we know ourselves, we're always home, anywhere."

With love from your most grateful older self,
Diane

~

DIANE SWEENEY WRITES FROM HER PERCH IN THE WOODS in Pennsylvania. She always thought her writer's life would be spent listening to crashing waves at the beach. But as she changed life, "home" found her listening to the chirping of birds, the wisdom of the woods, and the percolating sound of a bubbling creek.

As a curious copywriter, she enjoys working with a variety of clients creating web content, email series, ebooks, case studies and white papers. She does all she can to become the consumer of the product about which she is writing.

Her list of clients includes a senior caregiving franchise, a digital marketing agency, a mystery shopping company, spiritual advisors, life coaches, nutrition and wellness businesses, and an alpaca farmer. She is also the editor of her township's newsletter.

Her empty nesting therapy was started by blogging at her site Get Focused on Living. Intense therapy continued with writing her book called, *Finding Your Place (And Your Purpose) After The Kids Are Gone*, which is an ongoing project and may one day be published!

Connecting people and feeding them good food are among Diane's other interests. When not writing, she can be found in her kitchen, with her retired hubby, Don, creating meals for people they love, and for the homebound they support through a local charity, Aid for Friends.

WWW.DIANEMSWEENEY.COM

WWW.GETFOCUSEDONLIVING.COM

WWW.LINKEDIN.COM/IN/DIANEMSWEENEY/

WWW.FACEBOOK.COM/DIANESWEENEYBIZ

NOT-SO-SECRET
LESSON #6

YOU DO NOT HAVE TO BE PERFECT

~

As Laurie writes in her letter, "I think very often as women we feel like we can never admit failure and always must seem like we have it all together and are on top of our game..." We're the ones wearing lipstick and high heels calmly directing everyone to the lifeboats while the Titanic is sinking.

We believe that we must do everything perfectly and never fail. The problem is, our fear of failure keeps us from learning and growing. It keeps us from taking risks. And it keeps us from loving our lives, our children and our partners exactly as they are in this imperfect moment.

As the author Anne Lamott puts it:

"Perfectionism is the voice of the oppressor, the enemy of the people. It will keep you cramped and insane your whole life..."

Each of the women in this chapter felt the oppression of perfection. Each of these Titanides had to face her own fear of failure. And each of them found grace and acceptance on the other side.

As a young girl living in Argentina during a political coup, Serena learns that if you make a mistake you really could die. She grows up terrified to ever be anything less than perfect. It takes years before she finally understands that failure is not fatal.

For Chris it's her husband's brain tumor diagnosis that replaces her quick and easy confidence with fear. It's only when she finally stops pushing that fear away that she can find her way through. Because it's only when you truly feel that fear, that you can feel its opposites—hope, joy, and love.

Julie dreams of the perfect brilliant life only to realize there is no such thing. When she begins to choose her life exactly as it is, she can finally embrace her future. And it looks nothing like what she imagined.

In high school, Jennifer is determined to get As in every class, no matter the cost. She is so terrified of failing, of not being the best at everything, that she denies herself some amazing opportunities, and by the time she graduates, she is utterly exhausted. It is not until she's thirty-five years old that she finally lets go of her harsh, unforgiving inner critic and learns to be proud and confident in herself.

Lois is forced to confront the price of her perfectionism when, like Jennifer, Lois's younger daughter breaks down sobbing over a failed homework assignment. Lois reminds her younger self, "When you accept that no one is perfect, you will stop expecting your children to be perfect and you'll start doing things that make you happy, instead of wasting time trying to be perfect."

For Marcella it's her son's struggle with mental illness and addiction that forces her to finally admit defeat and stop trying to be the perfect mother. She tells her younger self, "You will no longer fear failure. You will become braver than you ever imagined. You will be vulnerable and soft and open. And you will fall in love with the world again..."

Do not let perfectionism keep you cramped and insane your whole life. Embrace the mess that is life and learn to love your failures.

1

SERENA SAVAGE

~

Every good thing is on the other side of fear.

AROUND THE AGE OF FIVE, MOST CHILDREN LEARN THAT IF they make a mistake, they won't die. When you were five, you learned that if you made a mistake, you really could die.

Your grandmother always used to say that the Savages had an odd kick to their gallop, and your father was no different. His job in the CIA took your family to Argentina in the mid-1970s when the coup to overthrow Isabel Perón was in full swing. He liked to collect political posters—graphic works of art plastered all over the city inciting people to action.

One day, driving through the city in your parents' sky-blue Peugeot, your father saw a poster he wanted to steal, which was (among many things) illegal. He got out of the car and left you and your mother parked by the side of the road, while he went around the corner to peel the poster off the wall. Cars idling next to buildings were often seen as bomb threats, so when a soldier on patrol saw your car, he started walking towards you, his gun coming up to point in your direction.

At the time, people we knew were disappearing. Neighbors vanished in the night. Our family pediatrician disappeared. When your father discovered people we knew were on the blacklist, he helped them escape the country before they were killed.

A soldier with a gun pointing at you was a very bad sign.

Your mother asked you to get on the floor of the back seat and covered you with her fur coat. She leapt out of the car and screamed your father's name. You had never heard fear in her voice like that before, and you have never heard fear like it since.

The coat muffled what you could hear, but the soldier was shouting at your mother, angry and emphatic. Your mother replied in a tone that was part panic, part *you-will-not-mess-with-my-child*. Moments later your dad came running back to the car, yelling to your mother. The tone of the exchange changed as you father started talking, the authority passing from the soldier to your father. The doors opened and closed, and the car started moving. Your dad turned around in the passenger seat, lifted up the fur coat, and smiled at you.

"We'll have to come back for the poster another day."

That was the day you learned that if you make a mistake you could die.

After that, there was nothing you feared more than making a mistake. If you took a bus and ended up in the wrong place—you could die. If you said the wrong thing—you could die. You obsessed about getting good grades at school. You never wanted to try new things because... what if you failed? You might die. And even when you did try new things, your fear was always there. It never went away.

Late in high school, your mom suggested you try failing a test, just to see what it was like. It didn't make any sense to you at the time. Why would your mom *want* you to fail anything? You didn't realize until much later that she was trying to teach you that the only way to learn *is* to fail.

After a gap year in Brazil, you went to Harvard to study

documentary filmmaking and bioanthropology. You earned both a Rockefeller fellowship and a Fulbright fellowship.

During your studies you got to work on a UK Channel 4 documentary about revolutions in Latin America, and went to the signing of the peace treaty in El Salvador. You climbed a mountain to a guerilla hold-out where rebels were still fighting, and for the first time, your fear matched the severity of the situation.

After many years back in the U.S., you went to work at the NASDAQ on special projects for the President and Chairman of the stock exchange. You were on your way to work—coming out of the subway to go to 1 Liberty Place—when the first plane hit on 9/11. That was the first time you felt the rest of the world feel the same fear you felt every day.

With experience, you began to understand that trying new things was scary, but that it was never that bad after you made it through the first few steps. So you began to try new things. But that fear was always there. Every new experience required you to push through that fear. It's exhausting.

One day, you decided to take a mindfulness course. That course, and the therapy that went alongside it, changed your life. One of the first things you learned in the class was the Metta meditation:

"May you be safe and protected. May you be healthy and strong. May you be free from suffering. May you have ease and wellbeing."

The moment that you heard the word safe, you began to cry. You never knew how much you wanted to be safe—to really *feel* safe.

And in this class, you learned about self-forgiveness.

When you heard your teacher speak about it, you felt like the light of the universe shone on you. In that moment, you realized that when you make a mistake, you can forgive *yourself*. It is only with this compassion for yourself and your own struggles that you can become whole, and free yourself of the constant fear.

Let this space flow over into each part of your life.

Don't pass judgement on anything you do. Whenever you begin to qualify anything you've done, STOP. Instead of trying to give an "honest" assessment of your work, leave room for other people to respond and to share the good things they see in your efforts. Leave space for what you have done—just let it be, and see how it is received. In every likelihood, you have done well. It's unlikely that you have failed, and even if you have... failure is not fatal.

So know that persistence in the face of failure is the key to progress. Know that you can forgive yourself, and that giving yourself space will help you become the person you want to be. Finally, know that every good thing is on the other side of fear, and that you deserve all the good that's coming to you.

So while you are huddled in that footwell, terrified under that heavy fur coat, know that you will *learn* to feel safe. I hug that little girl and whisper in her ear, "It might *feel* like you will die from your mistakes. But you won't. I'll catch you... it may take a little while, but I'll be there to welcome you, and make you safe."

Serena.

SERENA SAVAGE WAS BORN IN BRAZIL AND HAS TRAVELED all over the world. She speaks four languages. She studied filmmaking and bio-anthropology at Harvard and was a Rockefeller and Fulbright Fellow. She worked at Nickelodeon in New York City—her only claim to fame is naming Dora the Explorer—and then worked as Director of Special Projects for the President and Chairman of the NASDAQ stock exchange. After the market crash she did a degree in textile design, and when she moved back to Baltimore she was recruited to lead international training for Agora's International affiliates. She now works as the Copy Project Manager at Money Map Press.

❧ 2 ❧

CHRIS ALLSOP

~

When you don't know what to do, or where to start, just be willing.

DEAR CHRIS,

I'm writing this to you in the summer of 2010. It's hard to believe you began your copywriting business more than three years ago. You were so excited and so sure of yourself.

You didn't know it then, but your plans would veer off-course just as you got rolling. That your husband, Brian, would lose his job and start acting strangely, only to be diagnosed with depression.

You didn't know that the mistakes he made in his business, combined with his not working for a year, would nearly run your family into bankruptcy. And you certainly didn't know that after a year of trying to cope with all of this, Brian would finally be diagnosed with a brain tumor.

Now, I am writing to you, another year on. Brian's surgery was a success. He had only a few, minor side effects. But for you, the emotional wounds run deep.

The fast leap back to your business that you had anticipated hasn't happened. You are so buried in debt; you must continue your full-time job to keep your girls in university. Even your marriage is not the same.

Your confidence, which was once so quick and easy, has been replaced by fear.

You will try to ignore it and push ahead. After all, everyone tells you to think positive. Yet behind your smile, you no longer know who you are. You will resent the success of others. You will feel a pit in your stomach every time you look at your bank account. You will push yourself to work long hours, only to feel that you're still not quite making it. And you will be deeply confused by it all.

You don't want to hear this, but this is your journey.

This is how you will finally realize that you must stop pushing fear away. That every time you have feelings of anger, resentment, or self-pity, you are disguising your fear and sadness rather than facing it.

The day will come when you will learn to accept how you feel, in each moment. You will come to understand that you can accept these feelings, and then let them go, because the real you —your divine soul—is here and always has been.

You will also come to realize this journey has a purpose. Because it's only when you truly feel fear, that you can truly feel its opposites—hope, joy, and love.

So when you don't know what to do, or where to start, just be willing. Be willing to open, to stop in the moment and accept how you feel, and release. And be willing to keep trying, again and again. I can assure you: If you're willing, whatever you need to move forward will be shown to you.

For you are deeply and truly loved.

From your future self,

Christina

~

CHRIS ALLSOP IS A FREELANCE WRITER, SPECIALIZING IN financial, business opportunity, and alternative health copy. She is also a wife and a mom of three girls—all grown and out of the nest—as well as two cats who still live, very comfortably, at home. You can contact her at chris@chrisallsop.com.

3

JULIE HASSETT

~

No matter what is happening in your life
in this moment, choose it.

DEAR JULIE,

No dream you ever achieve will be as perfect and brilliant as you imagined it would be.

Not your home, not your relationship, not your career, not your children.

But before you take that as a depressing outlook on life, I'm writing to tell you it's anything but.

Because the biggest trap you can fall into is expecting that life should look a certain way.

You may begin to expect things your partner 'should' do when you have a bad day... things your boss 'should' say when you deliver good work... and things you 'should' feel once you accomplish certain milestones in life.

But when these things don't materialize, you begin to resist your own life... the very same life you built atop your biggest dreams.

All of a sudden, the life you 'should' have created is happening somewhere else. It's with an ex-boyfriend... or in a foreign country... or it's occupied with a completely different line of work...

STOP.

No matter what is happening in your life in that moment, choose it.

Actively choose it.

Choose the mess around you. It's there because you have been doing so many interesting things that you didn't have time to clean.

Choose the work you do. It makes your brain hurt, but you haven't set your alarm clock all year and you are finally free of an office.

Choose your family. Yes, they are mostly insane, but they are the mirrors you need in life.

Always choose yourself when you are alone.

Wholeheartedly choose every failed relationship... ill-conceived business plan... and every dumb 'could have gotten you killed' decision that turned into a great story you'll NEVER share with your grandchildren.

Choose every privilege and stroke of luck that has befallen you, and every hard-won success you've earned.

And then, accept that your future might look nothing like you imagine.

Choose a future that is both wildly unpredictable, and often woefully mundane.

Choose a future where you stand tall and in control, yet get knocked down regularly by harsh gusts of wind.

Choose a future full of rampant joy and cinematic moments, packed tightly with long stretches of ease and contentment.

I'm just saying that if you're going to dream... you're wise to dream big enough to make room for it all.

In real life you may create brilliance and perfection five percent of the time. But the simplicity, surprise and even heartache you endure during the other ninety-five percent is even more worthwhile.

Yours always,

Julie

JULIE HASSETT IS A FREELANCE COPYWRITER AND REAL estate investor. Her life, for the most part, has never looked anything like she imagined when she was growing up. Julie has been an actress in Los Angeles, English teacher in Europe, bait & tackle shop owner in Tennessee, and a Teletubby in Arizona. Currently, she lives with her partner (John), son (Redmond) and Chihuahua (Herbie) in Baltimore, MD.

For more about Julie, visit:

www.wonderhuntercopy.com

❦ 4 ❧

LAURIE TOBIAS

∽

Do not let yourself accept the victim role.

DEAR LAURIE,

Cherish the small moments in life. And understand your life is unique and even though you will go through ups and downs, dark moments and bright moments, successes and failures—these things are what will shape and develop you into the person you will become one day.

Embrace the good and the bad and use it as a learning experience. I firmly believe you do not get more than you can handle and often the darker periods are what will build you up and make you stronger.

At times in your life you will look back and reflect on the choices you made and it will become clear how your past has shaped your future. It is important to know how you got where you are in your life. Take time to reflect!

Always know that it is okay to fail—it is better to have failures in your life if you accept those failures and learn from them. You will grow so much by accepting those failures and looking at each one as a life lesson.

Do not let yourself accept the victim role. It is very easy to see yourself as a victim and take pity on yourself. You have control over your life and even though things may happen that you feel like you do not have power over – you have a choice how you handle and accept these things.

You should always believe in yourself. Be strong and confident and even if you do not trust that you can do something, if you show confidence, it will come across to others and they will believe in you.

Do not be afraid to ask for help and guidance. I think very often as women we feel like we can never admit failure and always must seem like we have it all together and are on top of our game. For some reason it is much more acceptable for a man to say "I have no idea," but as a woman we feel like if we admit we need help we are looked upon as being incapable of handling our role.

Unfortunately, often women do need to prove themselves more than men, but you are so much more talented than you realize. If you ever find yourself in a professional role where you are not given the respect or responsibilities or growth that you deserve, see if you can change the situation—if not, it may be time to move on.

Be a leader! Be someone that others look up to and do the right thing even if it is not the most popular thing.

Live your life with passion and remember you are so gifted and do not let your fears or anyone hold you back from doing whatever you want in your personal and professional life!!

Laurie.

～

LAURIE TOBIAS IS CHIEF MARKETING OFFICER FOR Johnson Brunetti. Laurie joined the firm in 2010 and her team is responsible for all the marketing in the firm. This includes digital, social media, direct mail, print, public relations as well as client appreciation events, educational events, referral events and workshops. She works closely with the Johnson Brunetti media contacts and partners. Laurie has also presented at Salesforce/Pardot events where she has discussed the ways that Pardot has helped the firm to develop some complex email nurturing campaigns. Laurie is always looking for opportunities to grow awareness of the firm in the marketplace among clients and the community at large.

Laurie lives in Connecticut and has two sons and one daughter. She enjoys running and biking and has participated in numerous races and triathlons. She strives to learn at least one new thing every day. She also loves to travel and volunteers to help underprivileged high school kids navigate the college application process.

5

LOIS MENTRUP

∾

Being perfect is an unattainable goal.

DEAR YOUNGER LOIS,

One of the biggest revelations of your adult life will bear down on you while you are sitting at your kitchen table.

You're checking over your daughter's math homework. But she doesn't understand the lesson... so she's done it wrong.

As you try to show her how do it correctly, she completely melts down.

Tears roll down her face, and she refuses to listen to what you're trying to teach her.

She simply can't accept that she didn't do it perfectly the first time. And that's when it dawns on you.

She's just like you. And it's holding both of you back.

You see, from a young age, your parents told you to always do your best.

What your parents meant was to always put one hundred percent effort into everything you do.

What you interpreted it to mean was that everything you do must be perfect.

But sitting in the kitchen with your daughter, you finally realize that being perfect is an unattainable goal.

Even more importantly, you realize it's an unhealthy goal.

It makes you afraid to try new things (you might fail!).

It keeps you from forgiving yourself when things go wrong (and they inevitably will).

It makes you defensive when people criticize you (instead of viewing that criticism as an opportunity to grow).

When you accept that you have flaws, the world becomes a much calmer place. You stop beating yourself up when you make a mistake. You stop wasting hours trying to eliminate every flaw from the things you create. And you start accepting criticism from family, friends and even clients without getting defensive.

Most importantly, when you accept that no one is perfect, you stop expecting the people you love to be perfect too. And that improves your relationships with your spouse, your children and your friends.

When you let go of your obsession with being perfect, you will naturally stop worrying about what others think of you.

You will start doing things that you *want* to do, things that make you happy, instead of wasting time doing things you feel you *should* do (like keeping a perfect house).

I will warn you... even when you are older and realize that you are not perfect, you will continue to struggle to accept this.

You will kick yourself for scolding your children unnecessarily.

You will still get upset when the first draft you send to a client doesn't completely delight them.

You will still struggle to forgive yourself when you think you have failed.

Accepting your flaws will continue to be very difficult for you. That's why I'm urging you to change your mindset *today*, so that maybe you won't have to struggle so much to accept your flaws when you are older.

No matter how much effort you put into trying to be perfect, you will never succeed. And when you accept this one simple fact, you will be a much happier person.

Yours,

Lois

LOIS MENTRUP HAS MORE THAN TWENTY YEARS OF experience in marketing and public relations (and more than fourteen years of experience being a mom). When she's not helping with homework, she specializes in developing marketing and public relations content—including email promotions, video sales letters, blogs, case studies and white papers—for clients in health, finance and technology.

❧ 6 ❧

JENNIFER DIFOLCO

~

Failure is not a dirty word.

JENNIFER,

When you were small, your mom will later tell you, you spilled apple juice on your favorite dress. Unlike other kids, who would barely even notice, you had a full-blown meltdown. Your dress wasn't perfect anymore, and you couldn't stand it.

And when you went to high school years later—the highly competitive all-girls prep school, where you knew no one—this perfectionism unfurled in full force.

You studied relentlessly, and got As in every class, but you beat yourself up *a lot* to get there. You were so afraid of failing, of not being the best at everything, that you denied yourself some amazing opportunities, and by the time you graduated you were utterly exhausted.

Your only respite was in your language classes. Professore Goethals and Señora Monford both put you at ease, with their joyful, non-judgmental approach to teaching. You felt safe in their classrooms, and their passion inspired you so much that you will decide to become a teacher yourself. After college you returned to your alma mater to do for other students what they did for you.

Eventually you will decide that teaching—a true vocation, if ever there was one—is no longer the place for you, and through a series of fortunate events you will find yourself recruiting for The Agora Companies in Baltimore.

And like teaching, recruiting is a calling. You will still get to teach, to guide and mentor. By helping people find a role that's right for them, you can change their future, and the future of the company and team they work with, too.

You will have to deploy every skill you learned while teaching, and more. A huge part of your work is building trust with candidates, creating a safe and non-judgmental space for them—just like Professore Goethals and Señora Monford did for you all those years ago.

You will have to listen, to learn, to lean in, and having worked so hard to overcome your own fears, you can fully empathize with theirs. You understand each candidate's resistance to uncertainty, their fear of the unknown, and though you suffered so much when you were younger, those experiences made you perfect for this work.

And finally, at thirty-five, you will discover *why* all the years of studying were so difficult for you—you will find out that your brain is wired a little differently to most. The moment you hear this, the missing piece of the puzzle will click into place and you will realize that it wasn't your fault that you couldn't concentrate like the other kids.

This discovery will push you to overcome the limitations you have placed on yourself, and to commit to really living. By thirty-six you'll be more excited and engaged in your life than ever before, because you will finally feel able to approach new situations and new people with confidence, without needing to control everything.

You will start taking bigger risks, attempting more in your work than you ever would have believed you could, and you will be so proud of everything you achieve. It's liberating, and you'll find a whole new world of opportunities and experiences opening up to you.

Sometimes you will still have fears about putting yourself out there, a fear of looking stupid or caring what people think of you. But when you take the risk—when you voice the idea, say yes to something you've never done before, or say hello to someone new in a crowded room—something good will always come of it.

So just remember, when the old fear raises its head and you are fighting to keep your eye on the future, that failure is not a dirty word.

Love,

Jennifer.

~

JENNIFER DIFOLCO IS THE DIRECTOR OF TALENT Acquisition at 14 West, an Agora Company. 14 West's appreciation for the importance of inspiration, passion, and personal accountability at work is evident in every interaction with its candidates and its clients at The Agora Companies.

❀ 7 ❀

MARCELLA ALLISON

❦

DEAR MARCELLA AT 46,

Tomorrow night your son is going to try to kill himself. You'll spend your twentieth wedding anniversary sitting in the psych ward. You'll discover he was doing drugs you've never heard of... so many drugs.

You'll wonder if it was the drugs that triggered his schizophrenia or if it was the schizophrenia that caused him to turn to drugs for relief... Who knows?

The next five years will be a death-defying roller coaster ride. You'll forget everything you thought you knew about love. You'll watch all your dreams for your son vanish like a deer in the mist. You will nearly lose your second son while you are so busy trying to save the first.

You'll fail at everything you do to save your family. You will finally admit defeat and give up all control. You will stop trying to be the perfect mother. You will make every mistake over and over again until you wear your failure like a scarlet letter on your breast for all to see.

You will be pounded by life like a meat tenderizer until all that is left is a fragile tender thing. Only then will you understand that love is the only thing that matters. Kindness is all you have left to give.

You will stand and talk with old people in line at the grocery store. You'll tell the waitress it doesn't matter when she forgets your order. You'll smile at homeless people and stray dogs. You will forgive anyone anything because you know that you too were broken and vulnerable once.

You will discover deep stores of compassion you never knew existed. You will no longer look for perfection in yourself or others. You will become softer. You will abandon all hope of fixing anyone or anything. You will simply love what is.

And just when you think you cannot bear it any longer, the universe will shift. Your children will begin to find their way. You will love them more and deeply because you know every moment of connection is precious.

You will no longer fear failure. You will become braver than you ever imagined. You will be vulnerable and soft and open. And you will fall in love with the world again.

You will use your new capacity for kindness, tenderness, and vulnerability and you will create community wherever you go. Because you will have nothing to lose anymore. No image of perfect to uphold. You will become real.

And your realness will act like a beacon drawing people to you. Suddenly you'll be asked to speak, to lead, to teach. Your business will grow. Your clients will tell you they want to work with you because you are so alive. You will see all of this as a gift and a generosity.

So tonight when that phone rings and they tell you your son is in the emergency room, do not give in to loss and darkness. Hold on to hope like a lifeline. You will find your way through. You will come out on the other side, braver, fiercer, more real than you were before.

You will become the Phoenix that rises from the ashes, fierce and bold. Hold on. You're a warrior. Fight!

Love,

Marcella

~

MARCELLA ALLISON HAS OVER TWENTY-FIVE YEARS OF experience working with successful entrepreneurs to help them grow their businesses. She was the business manager for Carl Solway Gallery, where she helped transform the small Cincinnati gallery into an international art phenomenon. As a venture capitalist, she worked with entrepreneurs and founders to help launch dozens of early-stage medical start-ups. As an entrepreneur herself, she built a successful direct response copywriting agency that works with some of the largest financial publishers, alternative health publishers, and supplement manufacturers in the country.

MARCELLA WAS AWARDED THE 2018 COPYWRITER OF THE Year, by American Writers and Artists Inc. for her outstanding performance record and impact on the copywriting industry. Her company, Copy Harvest, assists companies in maximizing their copywriting resources. Her clients include *The Motley Fool*, *Bottom Line, Inc.*, *Advanced Bionutritionals*, *Money Map Press*, *Natural Health Sherpa*, and others.

TODAY, SHE IS A TOP DIRECT RESPONSE COPYWRITER, AN IN-demand copy chief, sought-after mentor, and founder of the (Not So) Secret Order of the Titanides, an organization dedicated to promoting female entrepreneurs, marketers and copywriters.

. . .

For more information go to: www.MarcellaAllison.com, visit www.titanides.com, or email her at: marcella@titanides.com

NOT-SO-SECRET
LESSON #7

HONOR THE JOURNEY THAT LED YOU TO HERE

∼

In 1996, a scientist named Hans-Henrik Stølum discovered the formula for rivers. It turns out that there actually is a pattern underneath all that bending and twisting and wandering to the sea.

As writer and artist, Karina Bone said at the inaugural Titanides event in 2017, "After a lot of mapping and measuring, scientists figured out that every river will follow a path 3.1416 times longer than the shortest possible route from their origin to the sea." Rivers take their time, but they always end up at the sea.

The Titanides in this chapter have followed their own twists, turns and bends to end up where they are today. What they have discovered is that that wandering doesn't always mean a detour —it's a critical part of becoming who they are. And looking back, they have learned to love the journey that led them here.

One rainy night when Monica's old injuries are stiff and it's hard to walk across the room, her daughter asks her, "Do you ever wish it didn't happen?" In that moment Monica retraces the long road to recovery from near-fatal car accident: meeting the nurse who becomes her best friend, and introduces her to the man will Monica marry, and who becomes her daughter's father. So it's with a bone-deep conviction that she tells her daughter, "That night was a gift and certainly no accident."

For Jennifer, every decade of her adult life is filled with hard-earned lessons. Now on the cusp of fifty, she has finally learn that it's okay not to know. It's okay to wander. It's okay to wait and see what time brings you, because it's going to be okay.

As Bonnie traces her journey back to the beginning she tells her younger self, "There will be days that will make you wonder what you could have done differently. But set that aside. These mistakes will teach you, and as a result you will become strong."

For Arwen, it's a painful road to understanding that a man is not a plan. It's only when some kind new friends invite her to join them at church one day that she realizes the journey has been leading her here: to the understanding that it was a God-shaped hole she was trying to fill.

So as Karina told us at that first-ever Titanides event, "The next time you're wondering if all the wandering will take you anywhere, remember rivers... if you're rushing, you're not gonna get there faster. So just enjoy it; you'll get there." Honor the journey and trust that it will always lead you back to here.

❧ 1 ❧

MONICA DAY

～

Courage is not granted but forged.

DEAREST TWENTY-YEAR-OLD MONICA,

Tonight, your life will change. Dramatically. In fact, you will actually lose your life, and begin a new one.

As tempting as it is to make this a warning letter, to urge you to change course and avoid this pivotal moment—I can't do it. Won't do it.

Because this is the night you choose your life. And that choice changes everything.

Today won't be much different from any other day. You'll work long hours to earn your way through college. You'll have drama in your love life. It might be the 80s and everyone else might be addicted to cocaine, but not you.

No, your drug of choice is the elusive love of a man you can never have. And if you could have him, you wouldn't want him. Because if he wants you, surely there's something wrong with him. This is your disease. Your addiction. And it's as dangerous and costly as anything you might shoot up your arm or sniff up your nose. Especially tonight.

It will start with an argument about how he is keeping your relationship secret, when you want it to be public. You'll try to make yourself feel better by flirting with other guys, but it won't work. You'll talk to his best friend about it and cry for hours, but that won't work either (since he just wants to get in your pants too, silly girl).

By the end of the night you'll be exhausted, emotionally and physically. And then...

You will get in the car.

My love, no one wakes up in the morning expecting to be bleeding out in a field before their head hits the pillow again. No one gets in their car, expecting to fall asleep while traveling seventy miles an hour. No one imagines that a thousand tiny decisions will result in their having to pull themselves out of a crushed car, drag their broken body through a field of long damp weeds on a hot August night, flip themselves over the guardrail like a fish and hope that someone passes by and stops to help.

It's the kind of gruesome scene you see in movies. The kind of thing you read about in the paper. The kind of thing that happens to other people. But tonight, it will happen to you.

At some point, death seems like it would be a blessing. It will seem inviting and comforting—like going home. And considering how many times you pondered taking your own life during your tumultuous teenage years, it will seem like the best outcome.

That's when you will meet me. The woman you will become.

You will feel me rise up inside you. First as an energy and then as a voice you've never heard before, "NO! No. It's not time yet. No..."

And with that war cry, you will begin to fight for your life. Your new life.

For a decade or so, you'll refer to it as an accident, until eventually, you'll realize that it wasn't. It was a necessary step in becoming who you are. The lingering limitation in your mobility will be a constant reminder to slow down, to stop chasing everything and everyone. To let life come to you. To receive.

Yes, you'll miss the high heels. You'll stop dancing for a long time (but you'll find it again, and it will be the sweetest thing ever). You'll mourn the body you came in with, and the time you lost recovering while everyone else was graduating college, getting jobs, having babies.

But you'll gain so much more.

Years later, on a night when your old injuries are stiff, and it's hard to walk across the room to get a glass of water, your firstborn daughter will say, "Mom, you never talk about your accident. You never complain. Do you ever wish it didn't happen?"

You'll tell her the truth: No.

You'll explain to her that the mother she knows was born in that field. You'll drive her by it, like a sacred place. You'll trace the thread for her: the nurse you meet in the hospital, who becomes your best friend, and introduces you to the man you marry, who becomes her father. You'll show her the tree her father planted there during your courtship. You'll reveal all the mistakes and choices and victories that led to her birth. So she will know that regret is futile and courage is not granted but forged.

Your entire adult life will be a second chance, Monica... and you'll live it that way. With a depth that would have never been possible before. With an aliveness you might not have known otherwise. With a joy that courses in your veins, through every subsequent hardship.

What a gift. And certainly, no accident.

So much love and compassion,

Fifty-something-year-old Monica

PS: I will give you one piece of advice: clean your apartment before you leave. Because at any age, it's embarrassing when your parents walk in on your messes and have to clean them up for you while you're lying in a hospital bed.

~

MONICA ANNA DAY IS MANY THINGS—WRITER, producer, performer, coach, entrepreneur and instigator. She has taken a rich and varied life path and forged from it an approach to personal and cultural transformation that impacts every area of her clients' lives and magnifies their impact in the world. To find out more about Monica's story and her work, go to www.monicaday.com

❧ 2 ❧

JENNIFER WELLS

❦

Everything is going to be okay.

DEAR JENNIFER,

Every decade of your adult life has held some key lessons. Each one is hard-earned, but so powerful. These lessons will teach you that even on the days when your life feels like it's going to hell in a handbasket, everything is going to be okay.

THE LESSON OF YOUR TWENTIES

You imagined that you were in love with a boy. You moved halfway across the country to be with him, dreaming that you would get married and live happily ever after. Instead, you found out that he was a boy, and you spent a great deal of time taking care of him—paying his rent, doing his laundry, making sure he was fed.

A year and a half after you arrive, he walked in the door one day—a normal day, like all the other days—and you were hit with a wave of certainty that he had changed his mind about you.

To this day you can't understand or describe it, but it's as if you heard a voice, clear as a bell. You knew. But you didn't listen to that voice.

You spent another six months waiting, until he behaved so despicably that you couldn't tolerate it anymore. Not knowing what else to do, you called your sister. Your parents wouldn't help, and you were stuck there, having spent all your money taking care of him.

It turned out that one of the giant installation artworks from Marcella's gallery had just been dropped off an exhibit in Anaheim, California. The employee who delivered it had to come back through Albuquerque where you were, on his way to Ohio, where your sister was.

So he detoured, you shoved your stuff in his truck, and drove back with him to Cincinnati. He was lovely, and what could have been a traumatic escape ended up being a beautiful experience. And even though you have to live in Marcella's attic—not a finished attic, more like a crazy-aunt-Jen-is-haunting-us kind of attic—it was all worth it.

You learned to pay attention to your instincts—that fight or flight stuff is MILLENNIA old, so remember to believe it when your instinct says that someone is not who they say they are. When it feels like something is going to go wrong, like it's going to become toxic and you shouldn't do it, don't do it.

And you learned that just about every problem can be solved. Sometimes it takes the assistance of your big sister, but it can be solved. You learned to pick apart the big exhausting problems, break it down and break it down, until you had some small step that would move you forward. You learned that everything would be okay.

THE LESSON OF YOUR THIRTIES

When your sister was thirty-five, she just about blew your mind when she told you she was pregnant with her second child, nine years after the first. She was nearly at her due date when you jokingly said that since you hated your current job so much, you should just quit and take care of the baby. Your sister, who was working for some crazy-ass venture capital firm, said, "You know, maybe we should talk about that."

So you do. You got to witness the birth of baby Nathan (and hand to God, if they showed that in sex ed, NO ONE would have a baby ever again). You got to know what it feels like to have a tiny little thing that you are solely responsible for, and you got to have so many adventures with those two boys.

You loved the minutiae of parenting. Going to school, taking them everywhere—museums, the pool, we did crafts. It was amazing, and it was also the hardest thing you have ever done. You have to be present for children. It is so, so hard, and so amazing. You taught them so much of what they know. You loved watching Nathan learn, because everything he knew, you had taught him.

You worked twenty hours a week in a retail job so you could have the insurance to be able to do this—and the lesson that dawned on you was that you do not have to bear children in order to be a mother. You mothered all the young women that worked for you in that retail store, and you still have the beautiful cards they wrote you, sharing what they learned from you, and how much difference you made in their lives.

You are not a mother, and that is the best decision you ever made. You are not married, and that is the other best decision you ever made. Those choices meant that you could be the mother the children in your life needed. Even though you made mistakes and were so challenged, those children showed you again that everything would be okay.

THE LESSON OF YOUR FORTIES

When you stopped taking care of the boys in 2003, you had breakfast one morning with Larry Kavanaugh, who spent an hour telling you why he wanted you to come work for him, and you spent an hour telling him why you should not come work for him. It turned out that you were both half right.

You had never sent an email. You didn't own a computer. You had no cell phone. You had no idea what Microsoft Office even was, but you were going to manage accounts for a start-up that built ecommerce sites for catalogers in the mid-market—all of which might as well have been in Russian for all you knew about it.

You worked like a dog. You would get up in the middle of the night, unable to sleep with everything that needed to be done. You went into the office to work on weekends, and you locked yourself in that bathroom and cried more times than you could count, for six months. Your clients loved you. The people you worked with loved you. And you were so overwhelmed with everything you didn't know that you couldn't put one foot in front of the other.

Because you worked for such an amazing man—the kindest and best of men—you were able to take thirty days off to find yourself again.

In that brief respite, you learned that every person has value. You walked into a room with other people who were struggling and thought, "Sweet Jesus. These people are not like me." You were a total snob. But by the end of it, you had opened up to them, they had opened up to you, and they changed your life. They changed the way you operated in the world, because they were raw and vulnerable and authentic. They showed you that everything would be okay.

So when you came back to work, you realized that your value was not based on the minutia you had been drowning in—no one cared if you sent grammatically perfect emails or could create subtraction formulas in Excel. Your value lay in your unique ability to sell anything, and to create long-term relationships with everyone you came into contact with.

You realized, finally, that there was nothing wrong with admitting that you needed help, and that you sometimes had questions. This made you better at your job, not worse, and you breathed again, knowing it would all be okay.

A decade later, as you reached your fifties, the company failed. Now, for the first time since you were sixteen, you have time on your hands. Part of you thinks you should get another job in the same industry and keep going... but deep down you know you don't want to do that.

But you've learned that it's okay. It's okay not to know, and it's okay to take a risk.

So you learn how to embroider. You learn to can vegetables— you're Betty Crocker in the kitchen. You volunteer, to be out in the world in a different way. This leads you to working with the Titanides, and you meet amazing woman after amazing woman through the organization.

You plan events that people are still talking about a year later, and work on an incredible book. You are part of making these big things happen. And right now, even though you don't know what you want to do next, or what the next set of lessons will be, you do know this: you're a little less scared than you used to be, and you want to be a little more brave.

So, trust. Wait, and see what time brings you. It's going to be okay.

JENNIFER WELLS HAS OVER THIRTEEN YEARS OF EXPERIENCE AS a project manager and e-commerce consultant. She lives in Cincinnati. For more information, contact jenniferannewells1969@outlook.com

❧ 3 ❧

BONNIE SCHOOLER

∾

Don't ever believe you have to settle,
or that what's right in front of you at this moment
is the best you will ever be offered.

DEAR BONNIE,

How many times I have thought about how different life would be, had you known then what I know now.

Growing up Catholic in the 1950s, in a little town in Iowa, many things were not accepted, and there were rules about most everything. You are the youngest in your family, and as a child your health wasn't good, so your parents tend to overprotect you.

As you go out into the world, it is going to be a 'big whammo.'

Since I couldn't give you this advice sooner, you will make both really good and horribly bad decisions. You are going to make a lot of mistakes... but you will also experience life in exciting ways. Many opportunities will come along when you have patience and self-confidence.

My advice to you, younger me, is to think big. Be bold, and don't let anyone discourage you from doing what you dream to do. Believe in yourself.

Realize, though, that you don't know everything. Listen to people who love you, who have lived longer and experienced more than you. They are trying to save you from making mistakes you will one day regret.

If you are seriously considering getting married, take your time. Really get to know them. Get to know their family. Spend lots of time together, talk about everything that would affect a marriage with this person. Listen to the opinions of others, and seriously look at all the facts. Make sure there is a real love connection that will last a lifetime, and never be afraid to break it off at any point if you are unsure.

Don't ever believe you have to settle, or that what's right in front of you at this moment is the best you will ever be offered.

There will be days that make you wonder what you could have done differently. But set that aside. These mistakes will teach you, and as a result you will become strong.

Find out what is really important. Strive to live as fully as you can. Be the best you can be, both for yourself and others. Never give up on your passion for reading and the desire to write. One day you will have the chance to bring it to fruition. Hang in there, because everything is going to turn out.

Love,
Bonnie

BONNIE SCHOOLER HAS ALWAYS BEEN ENTHUSED AND excited about two things—writing and anything medical. She was a Certified Medical Assistant for over ten years in General Practice and Internal Medicine. She also worked as an

Administrative Assistant in a long term care facility, as a unit clerk in a hospital in Emergency, on a Med/Surg floor and in a rehabilitation facility. Additionally, she took care of an ill spouse for several years working with in home care and long term care providers.

Bonnie also was in Mortgage Customer Service in various positions for over fourteen years, knowing all things mortgage and she can certainly assist you with any questions you have about providing excellent customer service to your customers online, in emails, on the phone and in person.

Writing has always come easy for her, she has been an avid reader from a very young age, and always wanted to be a writer. When life got in the way, she saved it for her second life career.

Bonnie has studied with American Writers & Artists, Inc. (AWAI) under expert copywriters, such as Steve Slaunwhite, Charlotte Hicks, Casey Demchak, Nick Usborne, Sandy Franks, Will Newman, Joshua Boswell gaining her AWAI Copywriting Verification, Web Writing Expert status, COS (Circle of Success), Advanced Training and Professional Writers Alliance also through AWAI.

❧ 4 ❧

ARWEN BECKER

∽

A man is not a plan.

DEAR ARWEN AT TWENTY-FOUR,

Today you will wake up alone in an apartment for the first time. Who could have guessed that 'Ken and Barbie' would be getting divorced?

Everything you thought mattered—graduating from a competitive '4A' high school, your 3.9 G.P.A., being a champion athlete, looking so successful—will fall away. None of it will save you, or your marriage.

Right now, you can't imagine that you would ever regret the decision to bail on your marriage, but you will. Not for the first few years, but over time you will look back and wonder what could have been if you had stayed.

Having been intimate with only him would have been a great platform to stand on when encouraging your future kids. It would have shown commitment and dedication, and it would have eliminated money issues—entirely—for the rest of your life.

But as quickly as the money poured in from his success, the warmth drained out of the marriage. The void in your life did not shrink as you became more successful. Once you had money, you realized it didn't make you happy... and you found out the hard way that a man is not a plan.

And so you will shift your focus to something—and someone —new. You think that since your ex's money didn't make you happy, that maybe a new mentor will. But that bright, shiny distraction is only gold-plated, and not pure. He is a wolf in sheep's clothing, using you to boost his ego. But although it feels very dirty, very fast, something beautiful will emerge from this experience.

You have been actively, aggressively avoiding God your entire life. Your ever-preaching, Christianese-dripping dad had been unfaithful, couldn't hold a job, never paid child support, had gone to prison and was onto his fifth marriage before you were out of your teens. You always wondered if that's what God looked like—a volatile, inconsistent deadbeat who couldn't keep a commitment.

You will discover a different answer through sheer tenacity and your determination to learn, grow and understand. I love that you don't stop seeking.

At twenty-four, you have to start learning something you should have learned at fifteen. You have no friends, because they were all your ex-husband's, and your new challenge is to make friends, to maintain your relationships, and to learn how to be vulnerable.

Better late than never, and maybe it's for the best—the people you start to gather around you are loving, kind, business-minded and genuine. And they all love God, but the God they speak of sounds nothing like the God your father talked about. So you will accept an invitation to go to church with your friends, not realizing that your world is about to be blown apart.

That day, April 2, 2000, the pastor of a congregation of two thousand attendees will ask if there is anyone that wants to come forward and be prayed for. You will try your best to resist, and feel yourself failing. He will ask again, as tears stream down your cheeks and you hear your heart whisper that this is what you need.

You don't want thousands of people to see you walk to the front, but your fear and resistance melt away as you feel a strong pull, a sudden confidence that the void you've been running from is about to be filled. As you allow the pastor to pray for you, the void fills and you become whole. You no longer have a God-shaped hole, and see that no man, money, recognition or success could ever have filled it for you. From that day forward you will never think of marriage, love, money or success the same way.

Looking back you will see that it was all part of the plan. You had started working in a financial planning firm dedicated to serving retirees two weeks earlier, run by a very nice young man. You had earned a zoology degree, and wanting to work with animals, were thinking of this job as a temporary solution so that you could pay your bills—something you had never had to do on your own before.

Eighteen years later, that man is your mentor, business partner, husband and father to your three sons. Your presence in his life brought him back to a relationship with God, for which he is forever grateful and which has deepened your own faith.

At twenty-four you were so sure the dark, ugly beginnings were set in stone and would define your whole life. But God took it all and turned it into something lovely, impactful and glorious.

Nothing on this earth could make you truly happy, but through God you have been able to take your messy start and turn it into a message that impacts thousands of women around the world. Through your work, women who are struggling in their marriages, finances and parenting are inspired believe better for themselves, to take personal responsibility for their place in life and to understand that everything they need resides within them; that it's a God-shaped hole.

You got this girl!

Arwen

~

ARWEN BECKER IS A FINANCIAL ADVISER, NATIONAL Speaker and Co-Owner of Becker Retirement Group. Arwen has enjoyed nineteen years in the retirement planning industry at BRG, and as a fiduciary, she has the sole daily focus of leaving people better than she found them. After meeting with hundreds of ladies over the years, Arwen and her company has taken a direct focus on impacting the way women are treated in the area of finance through radio, podcast, books and she joyfully gives over thirty "women's only" events a year.

Because eighty percent of men die married and eighty percent of women die single, she has made it BRG's mission to help connect with ladies in her community who aren't getting the attention and help they need and truly deserve. She enjoys clearly identifying individuals' values, so making financial decisions becomes much easier. She lives for the "aha!" moment when people see how all their retirement assets, combined with expense, income, inflation and the unknowns of health care or spousal death, combine in a clear plan they can rely on for their entire life. Her deep desire is to answer that overarching question of each woman, "Am I gonna be okay?"

In 2018, Arwen was fortunate to be personally selected to partner with nine-time *New York Times* Bestselling author David Bach to assist in the recrafting of his wildly successful seminar Smart Women Smart Retirement™ based on the relaunch of the twenty-year revised edition of his million+ bestseller *Smart Women Finish Rich®*. Her astronomical success has earned her a position as a trainer for other female advisors nationwide to give this fantastic and educational event.

Arwen (along with her husband and co-owner Randy) is a proud mom of three incredible young men, and she takes pleasure in traveling, crafting, writing, serving her local church and enjoying their cabin on Harstine Island in Shelton, WA. Arwen is a lifelong athlete, currently enjoying early morning runs and long day hikes with her family and friends.

You can contact Arwen through her website at www. beckerretirement.com

NOT-SO-SECRET
LESSON #8

OPEN YOUR HEART AND
TRANSFORM YOUR LOSSES

~

When she was twenty-two years old, Cheryl Strayed lost her mother to lung cancer. In the wake of that devastating loss, Cheryl's marriage fell apart. Four years later, Cheryl decided to travel halfway across the country to hike the Pacific Crest Trail. She hiked over a thousand miles from California to Washington State. And she did it alone. And it was during those hours spent on the trail, testing herself mentally and physically, that Cheryl finally began to heal from all those losses.

As the memoirist and novelist says in her book *Brave Enough*:

"When you recognize that you will thrive not in spite of your losses and sorrows, but because of them... that you would not have chosen the things that happened in your life, but you are grateful for them... that you will hold the empty bowls eternally in your hands, but you also have the capacity to fill them... The word for that is healing."

The women in this chapter have known loss and they too

have learned to thrive in the face of those losses and to find healing.

Liz loses her parents, John and Jackie, in a tragic car crash. She comforts her younger self, "You will shed many tears, but you will also know great joy. The community you have nurtured around you in Seattle will save you; forgiveness will be the key to your healing. Writing will be the vehicle that gets you there."

Candice is orphaned at thirty-three, and she too turns to writing to help her through it. She tells her grieving younger self, "Losing your parents will turn out to be the perfect story for a writing competition. You will win the competition, land an amazing client from it, and launch your writing career."

Deb's father dies the day after her birthday and then four years later her mother dies the day before her birthday. Both of them managed not to die on her birthday, as if they were trying to save her from themselves. It's only years later that she is able to visit their grave and forgive them. She tells her younger self, "You think maybe you are just finally cried out, but you feel it in that moment. You could swear something moves in the universe, and makes room for good things to happen."

For Denise it is the devastating loss of the election that causes her to strengthen her resolve and commit anew to being present in the face of what lies ahead. She tells her younger self, "Have the courage of your convictions in the face of injustice, and in the face of the conversations that make your heart leap in your chest. Listen better, and hold true to your ideals."

Candice is only twenty-three, when she loses her mom, her best friend, her lifeline. But she uses that loss to fuel her fight for the World Wrestling Entertainment (WWE) Women's Championship. And when the title is stripped from her, she reminds her younger self, "The fight is never over; the magic is in the training. Always remember, Champions fight for their dreams, even when they seem impossible!"

The Titanides in this chapter have found a way to live in the face of these losses. They have found a way to hold the empty bowl in their hands and use it to create, to fill it up with words or tears or conversation. They have found a way to open up their hearts and transform their losses.

LIZ FARR

~

ALWAYS CHOOSE LOVE OVER FEAR TO GUIDE YOU.

NOVEMBER 2, 1993

Dear Liz,

Yesterday your parents, John and Jackie, were killed in a head-on collision with a semi whose driver fell asleep at the wheel. Today you're in shock. You're overwhelmed with grief and will be for some time. Today you're going through the motions of what must be done. Booking plane tickets. Arranging for a cat sitter. Informing professors and friends. Packing a suitcase.

What does one pack to wear at the funeral of one's parents?

This has already been a year of turmoil, and there is more on the way. In July you quit your job as a biochemist. In August you moved across the country to Seattle. In September you started graduate studies in linguistics. In October you ended a nine-year relationship with the man you thought was a logical choice for a soulmate.

This will be a year of challenges, of change. You will shed

many tears, but you will also know great joy. The community you have nurtured around you in Seattle will save you; forgiveness will be the key to your healing. Writing will be the vehicle that gets you there.

Listen well to the stories you hear of your parents and keep them in the treasure chest of your heart. Those stories will be jewels you look on when you need love. Someone will tell you to take your time letting go of your parents' belongings, and that you should take your time making those decisions.

Somebody else will tell you that people leave this world when their life's work is done, and it will seem like that when you go through your parents' house. They both always had projects going on—John with his woodwork, and Jackie's prolific crocheting, knitting, sewing and stained glass. It will seem like they had both just finished a project, and hadn't started a new one, which was unusual for them. Let that be a comfort to you, and you will treasure the creativity they left to you.

You will get through this year, and many more to come. Yours will be the scenic route, as John always described detours and delays.

Telling you now what the destination is will deprive you of the many experiences you need to get there, but you will use every one of those experiences in the end. It won't make any sense while you're on the journey, but every step is exactly the one you need to take next.

Do you remember the bright pink lipstick Jackie wore in the 70s? You despised that color for years. But now when you see that color—and you *will* see it, choose it, and wear it more often than you could imagine right now—know that this is Jackie sending you her love.

Your father John, so like a deep pool of still water, will be sending you his love anytime you see a still lake, an ocean, a pond. The still pools at the base of waterfalls are especially deep with his love.

Follow your instincts anytime you face an important

decision. That voice within you will never lead you astray, even when that choice seems illogical, crazy and impractical. Remember Jackie telling you that John respected you for being a risk-taker.

You will learn to prepare the vessel of your life for the serendipity and opportunities that emerge so frequently. You're a lifelong learner, and you work on improving yourself, trusting that it's going to pay off. And it will.

Don't be afraid to ask for help when you need it. Sometimes the most generous thing you can do for another person is to let them help you.

Always choose love over fear to guide you. Love is really all there is. When you act out of love, you will be a conduit to spread more love through the world. You need not fear that you are giving away a finite resource. Giving away love brings more into the world.

Don't be afraid to let your light shine. And know that you're never alone. John, Jackie and all of your dear departed loved ones are always close at hand.

Love,

Your older self

LIZ FARR IS A B2B COPYWRITER SERVING ACCOUNTANTS and bookkeepers around the world. She has also been a biochemist doing neuroscience research, a database designer and annotator, a back-of-the book indexer, a stay-at-home mom, and she even sold Herbalife before she became a CPA. As an accountant, she worked mostly in tax, but also performed audits, business valuations, litigation support, and cash-flow projections. After fifteen years as a CPA, she traded in her 10-key for a pen, and has been writing full-time since 2018.

She now uses her knowledge of accounting and tax to translate what accountants do into language that normal people understand. She writes web copy, blog posts and case studies for accounting firms and software companies, and articles for trade journals and industry websites, including the Journal of Accountancy and Intuit. She also ghostwrites for several prominent thought leaders in the accounting world, and those articles have appeared in *Forbes* and *Accounting Today*. She is currently ghostwriting a book for one of those thought leaders.

WWW.FARRCOMMUNICATIONS.COM

❧ 2 ❧

CANDICE LAZAR

~

You're going to be okay.

DEAR CANDICE,

It's early 2013. You've just gotten home from a consultation with a plastic surgeon.

And though you weren't sure it was possible, it is: you've hit a new low this year... and it's only March.

When Mom died, it was different. After battling illness for longer than you've been alive, she wanted to go. The end of her life was sad, but merciful. It felt like the way it should be.

But Dad's early exit six weeks ago is a gaping wound. His medical problems were more recent, and the severity of them was difficult to grasp. Dad wanted to live. He had plans for the future... an autobiography to write... a broken system he was battling within his industry.

Dad's death is tragic. And it has made you an orphan at the tender age of thirty-three. Sure, you're an adult, you have a husband, an apartment full of real furniture, and a graduate degree (with another underway).

But you're an orphan nonetheless.

Although you've decided not to be a mother, you sure as hell didn't choose to be nobody's daughter.

And now mere weeks after being forced into your new role, you find yourself questioning your whole identity in a new way, wondering how your appearance impacts who you are.

This upheaval comes after your husband accidentally rolls over in bed and elbows you in the face. The blood comes arching out of your nose so forcefully you think you hear an operatic crescendo. The white sheets are instantly transformed into a Jackson Pollock canvas.

When you manage to stop sobbing from the shock and pain, you slowly meander into the bathroom. Before leaving for the hospital, you want to wash off the trails of blood that have seeped through your fingers and run down your forearms.

You take your hands away from your face and look in the mirror. You see Marcia Brady looking back at you with her broken nose, prompting a fresh round of tears (and, admittedly, a fresh flow of epithets).

Which is where the plastic surgeon comes in. Now that a couple weeks have gone by, the swelling has gone down, and the doctor can assess you properly. Fortunately, it seems that only the nasal cartilage was torn, so the bone is intact. But your nose still looks kind of 'off,' and it feels asymmetric to the touch.

The doctor has bad news. "I can't just hammer your nose over a couple millimeters and call it a day," he says. Any change would require full-on surgery. "You are already very beautiful," the surgeon says, "but I would make you even more so by doing this, and this, and this..."

There's no black marker involved, but you feel like you're in an episode of *Nip/Tuck*.

Now you're considering the possibility of going under the knife. You never really thought about plastic surgery until this happened, but you also never liked your nose. You wonder if the

Great Nose-Elbowing Incident is an opportunity to make a change for the better—a blessing in disguise.

Wait... Don't do it!

Being newly parentless, your sense of self is already fragile. Imagine looking in the mirror and seeing a different face looking back at you. It would be a renunciation of your past.

Not only have you become unmoored, but now you would be the one choosing to do the unmooring. It's too drastic a move right now with everything you have going on emotionally. If you really want to, you can always do it later.

Trust me, you don't need surgery. Your nose will still feel strange, but no one will notice anything different about you. A few months from now, you still won't like it, but you won't think much about it.

On top of all that, losing your parents will turn out to be the perfect story for a writing competition. You will win the competition, land an amazing client from it, and launch your writing career.

Candice, you're going to be okay. You will feel lonely sometimes, but you will get through some of life's worst experiences as well as anyone could expect. Your life is full. Both Mom and Dad would be proud.

And I want you to know—though I am harder on you than on anyone else, and though I don't say it or even think it enough —I'm proud of you too, and I love you.

Candice

CANDICE LAZAR IS AN AWARD-WINNING DIRECT RESPONSE copywriter, marketing consultant, and content writer.

Before becoming a writer, Candice worked as an intellectual property lawyer. Her experience gives her a unique perspective on using proof to create a strong "case" for her clients' products and services. It also helps her write legally compliant copy from the very first draft, making for more efficient projects.

Candice writes primarily for the business opportunity and lifestyle markets. She has also worked with a number of financial publishers and B2B companies.

She enjoys live music, travel, Crossfit, and working on her website, www.cocktailspy.com.

For more on Candice, visit www.candicelazar.com.

❦ 3 ❧

DEB GRIFFITH

~

*Keep smiling. Keep the positive attitude. It is the armor that protects you
and that you pass on to others.*

DEAR DEB:

One day in your teens, your mother commented on how
often people told her that you were always smiling. Decades
from now you will still be known for your smile, and for your
positive outlook.

As a teen, under that smile, you ached for friends. You didn't
think you had any, but you just didn't have a *best* friend yet.
There were two girls in your school—J and B. They were the
very best of friends. You wondered why you didn't have any
friends like that, and wished that you could trade places with
one of them.

Throughout your school years, you wondered why you were
'born this way'—born different. You looked at B, with her blond
hair, and her smarts, and all her material things. You often
wondered what it would be like to be her. She said she wanted to

be an archaeologist. Everyone said that was cool. You said you wanted to be an author, and everyone just stared.

It will be a long time before you learn to let go of comparison, but when you do, your whole world will shift. Another big shift will happen when you discover your resilience.

You broke up with your highschool sweetheart after your freshman year in college. You left your alcoholic mother and your enabling father and changed colleges. The Writer's Workshop at the University of Iowa became your oasis... in fact, *all* of Iowa was an oasis, and you didn't leave for thirty-eight years.

Even so, you married a verbally abusive attorney, and divorced him a few years later—no kids, thank God. You did well in new jobs—ones that seemed to be created just for you, where the glass ceiling was a little thinner and broke when you tapped at it.

You found yourself in the police academy and went on to be a top-notch investigator. You married another attorney. You had three kids, thank God.

You discovered that you were exceptionally good at dealing with difficult people, but as a result you spent a lot of time dealing with them. They hijacked your life, and you paid for it with your health. For years you woke up to hands misshapen from arthritis and knees that felt like someone was pounding nails into them.

Your mother tried to commit suicide twice in your life. Your dad passed away first, leaving you in shock to care for your mother for the last four years of her life. It took you a couple of years, but you finally figured out that her death was actually her third suicide attempt. She stopped taking her blood pressure medication, and waited to die. She had a stroke first, and died at home in your arms six months later.

You will always wonder how they managed it, your parents. Your father died the day after your birthday. Four years later, your mother died the day before your birthday. Both of them managed not to die ON your birthday, like they were trying to save you from themselves.

Ultimately, you figured out that some people are just mean. They are high maintenance. They are trouble, troubling, and troubled. They go out of their way to be difficult, to ruin your hard work, your success, and your happiness. They try to wipe that smile right off of your face, saying mean things and doing even meaner things. The worst of them is your second husband.

You decide it's time to walk away, to lean on your own resilience, and so your smile stays. Your positive attitude carries you forward into the future you shape for yourself. And after this critical shift, things move quickly.

You go after that writing career that got derailed along the way. You start making films. You move. You get your health back. You swim, you take dance classes, you learn languages and piano and guitar, and all the time you keep smiling.

Eventually you will visit your parents' grave, coming to forgive them. You melt down. Your pour your heart out like you never have before. You ask for love. You ask to be successful in writing. You ask to be successful in filmmaking.

As you do, there's another shift. You think maybe you are just finally cried out, but you feel it in that moment. You could swear something moves in the universe, and makes room for good things to happen.

And they do.

A letter from AWAI comes, and through their program you learn to make a living as a copywriter. Later, you get an email from your highschool sweetheart. You haven't seen or spoken to him since you gave his ring back. He reaches out before a highschool reunion, and you reconnect. He has been through a bad marriage with an alcoholic ex-wife. He gets what you went through. He has three kids. He is single. You are single. Suddenly no time has passed and the two of you are very deeply in love.

Then an Emmy Award-winning television producer contacts you, and you go to work on TV shows. Your kids and your new love are very supportive. The scripts you write are produced and you earn film awards.

You marry the true love of your life at sixty-five. You celebrate the fifty-year anniversary of meeting your now-husband and your honeymoon in the same summer, climbing the Great Wall of China together.

One day, later in your life, you will think about B and wonder what happened to her. You will wonder if she is still in your hometown and look her up. You will find that she married her highschool sweetheart. She did become an archaeologist, and had a son. You will find a picture about her, but it will make you sad, sadder than all the times you wished you were her. You will find a picture of her tombstone. She never made it to forty, and you will realize that you would never change places with anyone else—never. Not for all the tea in China.

On that day you will be very glad that you are you. So keep smiling. Keep the positive attitude. It is the armor that protects you and that you pass on to others.

All those things that made you different when you were young are the things that let you move onwards and upwards every time that you need to. Many others want to make those shifts. But they are afraid. You were not, and you are not.

Young Deb, be glad that you're you. And always, *always*, keep smiling.

∾

I AM DEB GRIFFITH AND I AM A BABY BOOMER! I ALSO AM an award-winning writer. I recently married my high school sweetheart. We celebrated our honeymoon and our fiftieth anniversary climbing the Great Wall in China I graduated from the University of Iowa with a degree in biology and went to graduate school at Drake University in Des Moines for an MBA in accounting. I worked for the College of Osteopathic Medicine/Des Moines University, Wellmark Blue Cross and Blue

Shield of Iowa, and a neurologist during the last thirty years. I also worked for the Polk County Attorney's Office, was the police community relations liaison and was certified as a First Responder. I have written numerous magazine articles, Internet articles, infomercials, and presentations on health care topics.

4

CANDICE EHRLICH

∼

Remember that this is a marathon and not a sprint.

DEAR CANDICE,

Tomorrow evening you will lose it all. After a two-week European tour, a knockout will end your wrestling career. Soon the WWE Women's Championship Title will be stripped from you.

All the hard work to get there will instantly be taken from you as you are knocked out on live TV, in front of millions of people.

You see the journey that got you to become the champion is really only the beginning of your journey as a Champ.

When you lost your mom at the age of twenty-three, you were crushed. You lost your best friend and your lifeline, but in time you connected with her spirit. She guided you and together you fought for your dreams: you worked your butt off and eventually became the WWE Women's Champion.

You became famous around the world, starring in many Super Bowl commercials as the original Go Daddy Girl, and gracing the cover of Playboy. The notoriety will make you think that you have finally made it.

As it is stripped from you, remember that this is a marathon and not a sprint.

Painful as it is to have wrestling taken away from you, God will guide you into your next journey. Keep your eyes and heart open for the clues—it will become clear to you when you are ready for your next path. You will see that the devastating knockout on WWE Monday Night Raw was really a gift to you. If you could find the gift in that, you can find gifts anywhere, so remember to look for them in every situation.

Your Champ nature will be resurrected by the three beautiful daughters you will have. You will become a Champion mother, and as your children go off to school you will realize the real gifts are in the giving.

You will create a platform of inspiration motivating the masses around the world to feel a true sense of Importance for their lives, and you will fight shoulder-to-shoulder with them, helping them fight for their dreams.

Your life is a journey of training. The fight is never over; the magic is in the training. With no grit, there's no gold. Always remember:

"Champions fight for their dreams, even when they feel impossible!"

You are always loved.

Candice Michelle

CANDICE MICHELLE EHRLICH BEGAN HER LIFE WITH an unprecedented birth. Overcoming the odds, she grew up in Milwaukee, WI, where she was a true Cheesehead and Green Bay Packers fan. At eighteen, she followed her heart to

Hollywood to pursue her dreams of modelling and acting. She went on to become the first ever Diva search contestant to win the WWE Woman's Championship. From there she landed a dream cover and posed for Playboy. She is also known for her infamous GoDaddy.com Super Bowl commercials. After a career-ending injury, she went on to become the mother of three beautiful daughters. Her family is her greatest claim to fame, along with being married for half her life. While it takes a village to raise a child, it took her children to resurrect her as a Champion. She has a gift for creating Champions, living her truth and training her butt off. She is the Champ Candice Michelle! Contact her at: candicemichelle.com

❧ 5 ❧

DENISE FORD

~

Understand that disharmony is sometimes necessary to progress.

DENISE—

On the election night of 2016 you will stay up as late as your eyes will allow. You will go to bed anxious; holding on to a sliver of hope. The next morning when you wake up, before you even get out of bed, you will know that hope, 'that thing with feathers,' has flown away.

The fear that saw that man elected is similar to the fear you will feel now that he is the leader of the country... but you cannot live in that anxiety. You won't be able to breathe if you do.

As you prepare to go to work—to move on in the face of these results—you will strengthen your resolve and commit anew to being present in the face of what lies ahead.

In that moment, you will turn to your family, as you have done so many times. You will encourage your nieces and nephews, that their passion and fury is fair. You will dig up a poem—'Wild Geese', by Mary Oliver—in search of something to soothe your spirits, and theirs.

You will remind them, and yourself, to reach out to 'the other' to learn to listen; to listen to the fear and pain in someone else without judgment. Not to persuade, but to understand. Not to be 'balanced' or 'rounded,' but to create a dialogue.

As you've matured, Denise, you have developed an ability to diffuse explosive situations. You don't have the solutions, and don't pretend to, but you do have an interest in taking the dangerous emotions out of the moment, and creating a space where listening can happen.

You know that listening is an art form, and requires practice, but that the intention to understand is paramount and can create a profound shift in even the most difficult moments.

It's hard to do, to find the way towards love and understanding 'the other.' It's even harder in the wake of the hateful, divisive language that was spoken over our nation, over our families and communities. You know that words matter, and those words left wounds.

But you know, too, that words can heal, and in the aftermath of it all, your niece will remind you of the hopeful, buoyant words from Mahatma Gandhi:

"When I despair, I remember that all through history the ways of truth and love have always won. There have been tyrants and murderers, and for a time, they can seem invincible, but in the end, they always fall. Think of it—always."

Her hope will make you smile, and remind you that hope is essential to change, and doesn't have to disappear as you get older. It may diminish, but hope fuels our dreams and passions. It is nurtured by our friends, and you are so blessed by the friendships in your life—especially with the women you have known. Those deep friendships sustain you, and together you will try to find solutions that make sense in such a polarized world.

As Gloria Steinem said:

"God may be in the details, but the Goddess is in the connections."

You know this to be true. In building a community of people with your values, you have caught glimpses of that goddess many times.

So have the courage of your convictions in the face of injustice, and in the face of the conversations that make your heart leap in your chest. Listen better, and hold true to your ideal: to research, reflect and respond. One thing we can all do is to create a vision for ourselves—who we want to be in the world, and what we want the world to be for us and the people who come after us.

Continue to build the community that shares your values, and that holds you to bringing that vision to life. Understand that disharmony is sometimes necessary to progress, and accept that we are always changing.

You have no idea what's ahead, so find the part of your soul that recognizes that change is inevitable. Draw on the power and passion of our collective actions, our victories; allow yourself to be renewed and restored in the retreats, and always, always get back on the march.

Denise Ford

DENISE FORD IS THE CONFERENCE & EVENTS DIRECTOR for American Writers & Artists Inc. (AWAI). Denise has been affiliated with AWAI since 2002, working as a copy reviewer, the first Student Services Director, a product manager, copywriting coach, Events Coordinator and now, Conference and Events Director.

Denise works with a dedicated events team, who provide support for live and online event experiences for AWAI members. Prior to joining AWAI, Denise was an Adjunct Professor, teaching performing arts and theatre courses at several colleges and universities in the U.S.

Denise also enjoyed a celebrated career managing and directing theatre companies around the country including The Phoenix Theatre, Oregon Shakespeare Festival, A Contemporary Theater, Civic Light Opera, Asian American Theater Company and Playmakers Repertory Company.

In her spare time, Denise volunteers with the local community food bank, works with dog rescue—and can be frequently found in her garden.

NOT-SO-SECRET
LESSON #9

LET YOUR ANGER FUEL YOUR
SUCCESS

~

Nothing is more powerful—or more dangerous to the
established order of things—than a righteously pissed-off
woman. Which is why as little girls we are taught to stifle our
anger, play nice, and make the peace. It's the old double
standard. If a woman gets mad she's called 'hysterical' or
'hormonal'. She's considered a bitch. But if a man gets angry he's
called powerful, in charge, a leader.

In ancient Greece these righteously pissed-off women were
known as The Furies. They delivered social justice with a
vengeance, and there are plenty of women in the modern world
channeling that righteous rage. Think of Susan B. Anthony, Rosa
Parks, Elizabeth Freeman, and all the women who fought for
abolition, suffrage, civil rights, #MeToo, and more.

Our anger is a powerful tool. It feeds our optimism, fuels our
creativity and helps us solve problems. It focuses our mind and
moves us closer to our goals. And it pushes us to act, rather than
play the victim.

All of the Titanides in this chapter got good and mad at

injustice. They finally said, "Enough is enough" and decided to do something about it. They used their anger as fuel to change the world for themselves and for the women who came up behind them. They are the modern day Furies.

Kim is told over and over again by men that copywriting is really too hard a field for her and that she should just quit. But she doesn't give up—she chooses to believe in herself instead. She tells her younger self, "You are not going to let anyone tell you what you can or can't do. You know what you're capable of, so hold onto that knowledge."

Lorena tells her younger self, "Get angry. Stay angry. Make a list of all the toxic, misogynistic stupid things in high school, college, and work. See how they are failing you. Then blaze your own trail."

Sitting on a cooler sobbing, Abbey realizes has a choice, she can either listen to those who say she has no place as a chainsaw instructor, or she can become a warrior and prove them wrong. She tells her younger self, "The thing about glass ceilings is that there's only one way to break through them. Brace for impact and get ready to bleed. And holy shit, those cuts will hurt. But they will make you stronger."

For Patricia, the rage comes with the call-back from an entertainment agent who tells her "You're a really big girl. I just don't know how we will ever find back-up girls for you." That's when Patricia gets good and mad. She decides to produce her own fitness videos, knowing she'll never let the judgement and preconceived ideals of the fitness industry stop her.

Shannon is fed up with all the "mansplaining" that comes with writing in a male-dominated industry. But she doesn't let that stop her. She tells her younger self, "You'll learn to speak with a powerful new voice... one that isn't afraid to call it like you see it or put the small minds in their place..."

So go ahead and get mad. Get really mad. Get mad about injustice, about the people and things that hurt you and keep you down. Let your anger motivate you to act, to do something to change that situation. Don't stifle your anger: let it become a channel for your success instead.

❧ I ❧

ABBEY WOODCOCK

~

You will become a warrior, and no one will be able to question you.

Y OU'RE SITTING ON A COOLER, SOBBING.

For the first time, you've used your copywriting for evil. You tricked someone. Someone important. They believed everything you said. And now, in a classic be-careful-what-you-wish-for-type scenario, you're paying for it.

Next to you is one of your best friends, a logger named Jesse. Twenty feet in front of you, half a dozen drunk veterans are gathered around a fire, laughing and swapping war stories. Every time you hear a roar of laughter, you think they're talking about you.

Directly behind you is the kind of tent you see in war movies, filled with canvas cots. You can hear ten more male vets snoring inside. These guys are sleeping soundly even while the tent whips in the wind around them, confident they belong here. That's what your mind is telling you, anyway.

To your right are two one-man tents. In one is Vince, the Director of Operations of Team Rubicon. In the other, Jason, the Director of Training. The two men who—you're convinced —are going to put you on a plane and send you home within the next twenty-four hours. You stare at their tents and imagine what's going on inside. They each must be lying awake, trying to figure out the best way to break the news to you. *Sorry, Abbey. We like you... but you don't belong here.*

They had to have seen it. Every one of the people around you had to have seen it. You shouldn't be in this group. You weaseled your way in and now you've been found out.

This is the first cadre of chainsaw instructors ever in Team Rubicon, a new and revolutionary disaster response organization. Team Rubicon's mission is simple but profound—to take the skills of military veterans and first responders and use them to serve in the wake of hurricanes, tornadoes, and floods domestically and around the world.

Every person who picks up a chainsaw stamped with the Team Rubicon logo from now until forever is in our hands. It's big stuff. We all feel the weight of that. And no one more than you.

Among the group are combat veterans, search and rescue specialists, loggers, arborists, wildland firefighters, paramedics, a British paratrooper, and a sawyer climbing specialist (yes, a guy that uses a rope to climb a tree with a running chainsaw on his back). These are some of the bravest men in the world, with the most insane experiences you've ever heard.

Then there's you. This girl. This civilian. This... copywriter. And you're crying on the cooler.

You're *way* out of your league.

In the Internet marketing world, 'application only' means *"show you're committed by taking five minutes with this form and you're in."* Not here. The best sawyers in the organization applied— some who were pumped to be involved and some were pumped for the bragging rights that came with involvement.

Now, you were one hundred percent honest in your application—you were a proficient but not experienced sawyer. And you are a good teacher and passionate about the opportunity to be involved. You thought about every single word on that application, and used all the persuasion tactics you learned in your copywriting career.

You included the hopes, fears, and dreams of the training department, highlighted your strengths, and answered common objections. While those other guys provided straightforward answers to the questions, you had to sell.

And it worked. You were ecstatic when you got the email saying you were in.

The first day of training comes around quickly. We debate everything. Or rather, *they* debate everything. The merits of a reduced-kickback chain. Whether the ground-start or three-point start is better for beginners. Which type of tourniquet should be packed in the med kits. How to refer to that one part —is it 'bumper spikes' or 'felling dogs'?—or if a composite or steel toe should be required.

And that's just the classroom. At lunch it's whether or not Husqvarna is superior to Stihl. How many saws they own. The craziest, biggest, gnarliest trees they'd worked on. You have nothing to say. Nothing to contribute. You have no near-death stories involving trees. You don't even own a chainsaw.

That first day, your hands shake every time you pick up the chainsaw. Some of them notice. And even when they don't, *you* notice. Each time you make a mistake, you scan their faces for subtle signs—eye rolls, grimaces, snickers—and you manage to find them. Every single time.

So that night, certain that everyone knows you're a fraud, you drink. A lot. You're going to prove yourself one way or another, and that bottle of Jameson Whiskey is just the ticket. Surprisingly, this doesn't quell the voices in your head. And at 1 a.m., you lose it. You confess everything to Jesse. The application, your skills in persuasion, your guilt for being there, your embarrassment.

There's this phrase in marketing world that if you're the smartest person in the room, you're in the wrong room.

And while it's horribly overused, it's true. In order to grow, we need to push ourselves to get around people that have different experiences to ours. And it's not just about showing up to the rooms where the people are smarter than you. It's about showing up to rooms where you're the *only one* like you.

What they don't tell you is when you get in the 'right' room, it feels wrong. More than that, it flat out sucks. And it's scary. And it makes you feel so very alone.

Some of those feelings come from your own insecurities and fears. And some will come from *them*—the people that look at you and wonder how you got there, why you don't look or act like everyone else.

But you have a choice. You can blame them and try to change the system by demanding they put more people like you in the room. Some will agree; some will not. And some will keep throwing obstacles in your way, convinced that having people like you in that room means they may lose their place.

It would be great to say that your breakdown in the California mountains resulted in Jesse going back to the group and rallying them around you. That there was a big group hug, with those twenty men sharing their joy that you're waving the diversity flag, giving it a shot and encouraging women to rise up, lean in, and embrace equality.

And of course you have support. The majority of those men are on your side. And lord knows, Jesse tries to convince you that it will all be okay.

But as it turns out, it's not okay.

You have to work hard. You have to learn fast. But it never feels like enough. You can't shake the feeling that you don't belong. You look around and see faces that don't look like yours. The faces of warriors.

So you find yourself faced with two options—to listen to those that say you don't belong, or to prove them wrong. You decide to become a warrior, too.

The next year ends up being the most trying of your life. You have to prove yourself constantly: every time you walk into a room, every time you pick up a chainsaw. Sometimes you're proving yourself to others, sometimes to yourself. You have to stand in front of people who are more qualified, more experienced... and teach. You have to adjust your approach knowing that you're going to be questioned more than anyone else will be.

You have dozens of calls with leadership addressing your right to be there. You buy a chainsaw, practice your skills, and work with Jesse almost daily by calling him with questions, texting photos of felled trees to analyze, and travelling across the country to cut every tree they'll let you.

But it's not Jesse's battle to fight. And he can't win it for you.

You do everything you can possibly think of to prove yourself. To stop the questions both coming from the mouths of your co-instructors and from your own head. Good is not good enough. You have to be the best.

And six months later, you're asked to teach the first field certification class in the history of the organization. On your own.

On your way there, during a layover in Chicago, your phone rings. It's one of the guys who had seen you sitting on the cooler six months earlier. You smile, expecting some words of encouragement. Instead you hear:

"Abbey, I just want to let you know that I and a few other guys have been talking. We have zero confidence in your ability to teach this. We are petitioning the organization to stop chainsaw use on this operation while you're there. Just thought you should know."

Those words echo as the flight lands. And they come up

again just before you teach the class... because he keeps saying them to anyone who will listen. You feel sick to your stomach as you stand up to teach the class, his words still deafening in your ears.

But you run the class perfectly, and you become the first of your group to certify chainsaw operators directly in the field. You certify nineteen of them, in fact, and they go on to serve the flood-stricken community of Wimberley, Texas. Our National Operations, Training, and Leadership teams are thrilled as we begin to usher in a new era of disaster response, and you quietly chalk it up as a win.

You go home and write the manual on how to best run a field certification class. And you keep teaching. You fly from Omaha, Nebraska, to Fort Collins, Colorado to Newton, New Jersey to cut more trees, teach more classes. Of the first hundred or so sawyers to be knighted by Team Rubicon, you're directly involved with around sixty of them.

Finally, in June of 2016, you personally train Bekah, the second female chainsaw instructor. Today, there are half a dozen women throughout the country teaching classes and hundreds running saws. They don't have to fight anymore. Because *you* took those bullets. *You* have the scars.

THERE'S A LOT OF TALK IN COPYWRITING AND OTHER industries about encouraging diversity and inclusiveness. But there's not much talk about how that actually happens. When you look back in history in various industries, you'll see stories that mirror your chainsaw story. Stories about the first.

When you're running point—a term you learned from the veterans on that mountain—you're the first in the patrol, the one that walks into the unknown. And for you, that meant taking the incoming fire and cutting a path that the women of Team Rubicon could follow you down.

You can't wait for someone else to fight your battle, or for the enemy to stop firing, or for the war to stop. The only thing to do is to step forward, take real action, and lead the charge. You have to walk out blindly and take the fire to protect those behind you. And it sucks. And it's hard. And it tests you.

But we all have to decide which battles we are going to fight. If there's a cause you want to advance there's no easy way to do it. You have to take the fire. No one will fight your battle for you. Only you can do that.

The thing about glass ceilings is that there's only one way to break through them. Brace for impact and get ready to bleed.

And holy shit, those cuts will hurt. But they will make you stronger.

There's always going to be something to hold you back. The way you look. Your gender. Where you're from. Your experience. We all have our obstacles. And that can be limiting or it can be a source of incredible strength. By struggling through those battles and overcoming those obstacles, you'll earn the scars and learn the lessons that others won't have to, and progress will follow. In the process you'll get stronger, fight harder, and be better.

So when you're crying on that cooler on the side of a mountain, know this: you will become a warrior too, and no one will be able to question you.

~

ABBEY WOODCOCK HAS BEEN A DIRECT RESPONSE copywriter since seventh grade when she wrote a thirty-page sales letter asking her crush to the dance (with dismal results). Since then, she's converted better... writing sales pages and emails you've probably read from some of the biggest names online. Now she teaches those skills at the Business of Copy.

PATRICIA FRIBERG

~

You don't let anything stop you, and you won't let anything stop them either.

TO LITTLE PATRICIA—

When you were eight years old, if you weren't hanging upside down, you were perfecting your cartwheels. You loved gymnastics.

The day your mom came home and told you she had signed you up for gymnastics, you were thrilled... not least because she also bought you the most beautiful leotard you had ever seen. It was the most gorgeous shade of fuchsia, with cap sleeves and ruching in the center.

The day of your first competition, you walked into the gymnasium in that pink leotard and got a rush when you saw that it was wall to wall with people, all the way around. You completed your first round on the balance beam, and it was flawless. You didn't even stumble.

Then it was time for your floor routine. As you stood in the corner of the mat, arms raised in full presentation mode in front of the judges, you could not believe the rush you got, knowing that so many people would be watching your cartwheels, *finally*!

You ran as fast as you could and dove into a dive roll... but with all that speed the dive turned into a full flip and you landed —BANG—on your back. The crowd let out a huge gasp and then went completely silent.

As you lay there, getting your breath back, two choices flashed through your mind. You could run over to Mom's lap and hide, which you wanted to do so badly... or you could get up, like all the Olympic gymnasts you loved to watch on TV, and keep going. The roll had not gone to plan, but the show had to go on, so you got up, and continued.

You didn't let the fall stop you.

About a week after the competition, your coach said, "*Tricia, you are getting too tall for gymnastics. Perhaps you should consider another sport, like basketball.*"

You were devastated, but dutifully took your spot on the basketball team, playing forward. You would run up and down the court dribbling the ball... up and down, up and down, up and down... but all you could look at were the cheerleaders. All you could think was how desperately you wanted to be there instead. You didn't want to be shooting boring baskets, you wanted to be there on the sidelines, doing your tricks!

So you decided to try out for cheerleading... but you did not make the squad. You did, however, get offered a place as the Bulldog Mascot. You would put on that furry suit, with the big furry feet and the giant furry Bulldog head (and if you did a flip in *that* thing and landed on your head, you were totally fine). It wasn't what you'd had in mind, but you got to be there on the sidelines with the cheerleaders, doing your tricks, and it was fabulous.

You didn't let the suit stop you.

Flash forward about twenty years, after you got your therapy degree and fifteen years of experience in the fitness industry, you and your husband moved to sunny SoCal from Chicago. Soon after, you started getting recruited to appear in fitness DVDs.

Hooray for Hollywood, right?

The first call-back went a little something like this:

"Hi Patricia, it's Ariana. You know, we really love your work... but you are a really big girl. I just don't know how we will ever find back-up girls for you."

Wow. You had never been told anything like that before... and worse, Ariana sounded like she was just flipping her hair and examining her nails while she dropped that one on you.

The next few conversations all sounded very similar. One person even told you not to go off and get pregnant because your time would be here soon.

Then one afternoon, you got The Call.

It was from the largest fitness DVD company in the world. They were in every store—from Whole Foods to Target and everything in between. Becky, the producer, sounded so excited: *"Patricia, you're our girl! We can't wait to feature you in our next DVD, you are perfect for this."*

You took a deep breath, thanked her for the opportunity, and let her know that you were five months pregnant.

She paused for a long moment, and then said: *"Oh... well, we can't put you in front of the camera for an Abs DVD,"* and hung up.

This lit a fire under you. Six months later you had produced your own pre-natal DVD. You created, choreographed, directed and starred, because you wanted every pregnant woman to feel beautiful not matter their shape or size. Again, it was not how you expected things to turn out, but this was the inception of Belly Beautiful Workout, and you went on to create four more DVDs after that—all award winning programs that have been featured in media all over the country.

You didn't let the Arianas or the Beckys of the fitness industry stop you.

More recently, you were up for a promotion in one of the most reputable fitness brands in the country. You were in the running to become the West Coast Ballet Barre Ambassador, and several people were being considered for this job. After your audition tapes and interviews, the feedback was that you needed to move more elegantly and have a deeper knowledge of ballet if you were going to have a shot at the role.

You said yes. You would be elegant! You immediately found the best ballet teacher in your area and studied with her intensively, every day, for months. And let me tell you, *she was a hard-ass*.

But you got that job. You became the West Coast Barre Ambassador and continue to take ballet classes with your hard-ass teacher to this day. You absolutely love ballet—you get to wear a pink leotard! No one minds how tall you are, and several months ago you were even given your very first pair of pointe shoes.

You didn't let ballet stop you.

So now every Monday, you take off your pointe shoes, pull your leggings over your tights and pink leotard to rush off to teach your barre class. As you look around the room filled with students your role becomes very clear. Your job, as a fitness professional, is to make every single person in that room—no matter, their shape, size, gender, age, injuries or limitations—to feel comfortable and successful.

You don't let anything stop you, and you won't let anything stop them either.

PATRICIA FRIBERG HAS BEEN MOTIVATING STUDENTS FOR over twenty years. She is known for her ability to challenge her clients in a warm and encouraging manner, leaving them inspired and prepared to achieve their goals. She has taught a variety of group and individual formats in premier clubs in New York, Chicago, and Los Angeles, and has also taught for Harpo Studios in Chicago. More recently, she has begun teaching online for FitnessGlo. Patricia teaches a variety of formats including; pilates, cycle, barre, corrective exercise, conditioning, and myofascial release. She currently teaches classes in southern CA, where she also has specializations in pre/post natal rehabilitation, breast cancer survivorship, and several sports-specific indications.

She is the creator of the award-winning prenatal and postnatal fitness DVD series Belly Beautiful Workout. She was awarded the "Producers Choice Award" by 208 Entertainment INC and is the fitness expert for the JAM School Program and The JAM World Record Event, bringing fitness breaks to school children across the globe. Patricia also holds a master's degree in art therapy and clinical counseling, and has worked with intensive outpatient programs for multiple populations, including those with eating disorders and in need of weight management.

❧ 3 ❧

SHANNON HOUSLEY

∼

You are an unstoppable force.

DEAR YOUNGER SHANNON,

I want you to know that writing in a male-dominated industry is no easy task. There will be days when you feel like you've broken into the coveted boys club... only to get smacked right in the face by someone who feels the need to do some "mansplaining."

Just shrug it off and let it slide right down your shoulders. You are an unstoppable force. No small-minded male is going to stand in your way, and it won't take long before you start to discover that these unpleasant occurrences have toughened you up.

Your newfound 'balls' and formidable presence will in turn cause the put-downs or talk-down-tos to occur less frequently.

Not only that, you'll find that you will learn to speak with a powerful new voice ... one that isn't afraid to call it like you see it or put the small minds in their place. After all, you are no ordinary, run of the mill, stand-there-and-take it female.

And not only do you belong in the boys club, you are going to give them one helluva run for their money.

So just get out there and show them exactly what it means to be a girl.

Shannon Housley

~

SHANNON HOUSLEY IS A MARKETING STRATEGIST AND Financial Copywriter. Beginning her copywriting career with an award-winning options investment research firm as the Senior Marketing Editor, she managed and copychiefed a team of freelance copywriters, analyzed metrics, created campaigns, and worked closely with C-level executives to exceed revenue goals.

Prior to copywriting, she was a Compliance Officer for a Registered Investment Adviser with nearly $3 billion in assets under management. This SEC compliance regulation experience allows her to write compelling sales copy that won't get tangled up in the Legal Department's red tape... which can be a huge timesaver when trying to hit campaign launch deadlines.

Since starting her own marketing consulting business as a strategist and copywriter, she's had the pleasure of creating video sales letters (VSLs), direct mailings, web content, landing pages, banner ads, autoresponder email series, etc. for numerous publishers.

When she's not writing, you can find her travelling the country with her husband, riding her Harley, and riding her off-the-track thoroughbred as well.

❧ 4 ❧

LORENA BUENO

~

The little pebbles we're kicking down the hill today will start the next avalanche.

Dear Lorena,

Thirty hours ago you burst into tears at a table full of strangers. You're used to tears, but usually it's not because you read a prompt to talk about what you have in common with the analytic genius of Ada Lovelace at your first Titanides convention.

Thirty years ago, your English teacher made you mad, and you cried at your table then too. The only fun assignment that year had been to write your own myth. You read yours aloud, and the teacher inaccurately called you out for plagiarizing—completely ignoring the kid who copied out a Kipling in full.

That was the first moment you let your anger seep in, to get you, to let it stoke your flames. Your anger is a tool that will serve you well. It makes you stubborn, and it will drive you to forge past everything people say you cannot do.

So get angry. Stay angry. Make your 'impossible lists' of things you want and keep it in your heart pocket.

Take this critical moment—the anger, the embarrassment, the injustice of it—and make a list of all the stupid things you're going to reject in the toxic and misogynistic culture you encounter in high school, college, traditional jobs and hobbies.

And by all means, try those places a while. Analyze how they're failing you, and then blaze your own trail.

Because you're going to see it everywhere. The toxicity spills out from the very architecture of the workflow we push through every day. From societal expectations to actual differences on how we're treated, women have a lot to fight against, and that can be exhausting and isolating.

That's why when you get the chance to get around great women—like the ones around the table when Ms Lovelace set you off—you should leap at the chance.

You will see your experiences echoed in their experiences, and realize that it's not about you. There's nothing wrong with you. *Everybody* is getting some kind of pushback, but not everybody is just going along with the flow. Stick around the people chipping away at the status quo.

Recently you read a quote that said:

*"Everybody worries about going back in time and making a small change that disrupts everything, instead of thinking about what small changes they could make **now** that will disrupt everything."*

It's a shift to think about the current struggle we are facing that way. It might seem like we're making unbearably slow progress, but the little pebbles we're kicking down the hill today will start the next avalanche.

In the meantime, take that need to geek out and analyze everything to turn it into a career. It pays well, and you get to measure people's expectations, then blow their milestones right out of the water. Learn to 'bring the awesome' at every turn, and let people talk, so you can figure out what makes them tick, how they got where they are, and how you can do the same, in your own way.

Listen to the lunatics above you, so you can surpass them and keep any lunatics you get under you from driving you crazy with their bullshit. Don't play the one-up game—they only play it because they have to feel they are better than you at something. It's not a lot to let them have that small victory. Let your rage become a channel for your success instead.

Follow your purple pen and keyboard to a much more enriching life. It's gonna hurt at times, but each time it does, you will learn something. Follow the wandering trail to your own kind of life and your own kind of peace. There's no wrong way to be when you're blazing your own trail.

Wear your sweaters inside out and don't put your pants on one leg at a time like everyone else. And if someone doesn't like it, kill 'em with competence and let 'em die mad about it.

Lorena.

LORENA BUENO is a Senior Information Developer and Technical Writer, specializing in SaaS technology. She has extensive experience in technical content writing, process and task analysis, content strategy, explainer videos, and email campaign creation.

She's a seasoned writing professional with a strong track record of creating robust, comprehensive technical and educational content for a variety of audiences in platform-independent formats for both online and offline consumption in waterfall or agile development environments.

http://www.linkedin.com/in/lorenab

5

KIM KRAUSE SCHWALM

~

To love and believe in yourself is basic self-care.

To you, you fabulous, awesome woman—

Life is about being resilient.

You need to be able to take risks—and fail spectacularly sometimes.

You need to be able to deal with the harshest of criticism—and let it roll off your back.

You need to be able to handle the ups and downs—even when there are a lot more downs than ups—and never, ever, ever give up.

You need to learn the valuable lessons in your failures and hardships, see them for the gifts they are, and turn them into opportunities.

More than anything, you need to believe in yourself. And you do.

You were extremely fortunate to work at a direct response

company called Phillips Publishing. Bob King, the publisher of the consumer division, was one of your most influential mentors, as he was for many people in the direct response world.

Phillips was an incredible company. Bob's attitude was that if you weren't failing, you weren't trying enough new things. You were expected to write up your marketing lessons every month—and share them with your colleagues—about what you had learned from your failed campaigns.

That taught you not to fear failure, and to keep trying new things until you found a winner. That lesson has served you throughout your whole life, because it showed you that when you don't get crushed by your mistakes—but learn from them instead—you eventually get to that next breakthrough.

When you first came to Phillips Publishing, after seven years of marketing success at Blue Cross and Blue Shield, you were asked to join their new 'Special Products' division. In this role, you scouted out new products to promote to the back-end of a highly successful health newsletter, and wrote the copy for each test promotion. You had some big winners, and some huge flops, but it was all about learning what this emerging alternative health market wanted.

One of your greatest lessons was that this market wanted a particular doctor's nutritional supplement line. Three months later, you led the launch of not just his supplement line, but an entire separate subsidiary of the company, which you helped grow to $23 million in annual revenue within three years. You were barely thirty-two years old, leading this huge division, and feeling on top of the world.

But that was not to last.

The company's Board of Directors starting putting pressure on, asking why a young woman with no experience in the nutritional supplement industry was leading such a lucrative project. They hired an older guy from the supplement space to replace you.

You had worked so hard, and had been very successful, and

the response was to bring in a man—with no marketing experience—to take it over from you.

That did not go well.

When you eventually ran out of patience and moved to another division, things came apart at the seams. After a week, the Board of Directors realized you had been propping him up, and he was out.

Around this time your father was diagnosed with a very aggressive prostate cancer, and you had recently found out you were pregnant with your first child. You were so hopeful that he would live long enough to meet your child, and spent as much time with your father as you could.

He was a very smart, supportive guy and having a close relationship with a father like that was very empowering for you. It gave you a certain immunity to the "BS" that other men were about to bring down on you.

You had spoken with your dad many times about the freelance copywriters Phillips hired, and he suggested you give it a try after the supplement division was taken away from you. It was some of the best advice he gave you, and some of the last.

He did not make it long enough to meet your son.

The very next day after your father passed away, you found out that your husband's mother had pancreatic cancer. She died three weeks later. You and your husband were in a fog of grief; it was an extraordinarily hard time, made even more difficult by the uncertainty and frustration with your career.

But when your son was born he looked just like your dad. The shape of his face, the eyebrows, it was all him. And two years later when your daughter was born, she looked just like your husband's mom. Seeing your parents live on in your children helped you heal.

Bob King came to your father's funeral—that's the kind of company Phillips was. (And recently it was your turn to attend Bob King's funeral.) The people that founded and led Phillips were great people, so it was very difficult when you went back to work from your first maternity leave and found that your division leaders didn't seem to know what to do with you.

When you left, you were riding high. You were one of the rising stars of the company, with your pick of projects to work on. But upon your return, you got "mommy-tracked".

You were moved from an outside office to an inside office, your executive furniture was shrunk down to almost nothing, and you felt like you were being pushed out.

You spent your work breaks pumping breast milk in the bathroom, and sometimes broke down crying in your office (at least you still had a door to shut), trying to figure out what had gone wrong. Here you were at such a happy time in your life, and you found yourself grieving for your career.

Eventually, one exhausting day, your dad's advice came back to you, and you decided to take the leap into copywriting. You had gotten the experience, you had written copy in an unofficial capacity for years for in-house projects, and you knew deep down that you could do it.

You had seen the lifestyle the top copywriters lived... the income potential... the flexible hours... the ability to work twenty hours a week and make two to three times (or more) what you were making as a marketing executive working fifty-plus hour work weeks.

There was a gentleman who had a supplement business right near where you lived, and he brought you on for a six-month retainer arrangement, which guaranteed ninety percent of your current salary in exchange for twenty hours a week, or half your time.

That meant you could keep your nanny, focus on building your freelance copywriting business, *and* see your infant son throughout the day.

You were able to bring on other clients right out of the gate, and in the first year you made fifty percent more than you had been making at your six-figure job the year before.

Eventually, Phillips will become one of your best and biggest clients, and you will work freelance with them for years to come —a good lesson not to burn your bridges.

One day you will visit the Phillips offices and run into two senior male copywriters. They will ask what you're working on, and turn up their noses at the projects you mention.

They will tell you that copywriting is really too hard a field for you, and that it would be easier for you—and your family—if you stayed in a more regular role.

You will tell yourself they were either joking around, or that they didn't want the competition. Either way, you will choose to believe in yourself and not to allow their insecurities to stop you.

You will have to decide this all over again when you run into another man at a publisher's conference a few years later who asks how old you are—thirty-seven—and proceeds to tell you that the best copywriters are men, and even they don't get good until they're in their late forties or fifties.

Both of these were the same old attitude over again.

A young woman surely can't run the $23 million business she built from nothing! We need an old white guy! A young woman surely can't write good copy! We need an old white guy!

Well, young Kim, we've been there, done that, and you are not going to let anyone tell you what you can or can't do. You know what you're capable of, so hold onto that knowledge.

We all know deep down that we have something that's special, and something that we love about ourselves.

Try to remember that, go back to it, give yourself some love and affirmation. Try not to seek it from other people—it has to come from yourself. To love and believe in yourself is basic self-care.

Remember that it's okay to fail before you succeed... in fact, it can be a good thing. So stay strong. Stay resilient. Keep learning. And always, always believe in yourself.

Kim Krause Schwalm.

~

KIM KRAUSE SCHWALM WAS ALWAYS A MARKETER WHO could write copy. She spent more than thirteen years in the corporate world in various marketing positions—from Brand Manager to Publisher to launching and running the Healthy Directions supplement business and growing it to more than $23 million in sales within three years—before she started her freelance copywriting career in 1998.

Now more than two decades later, Kim has built a reputation as one of the top A-level direct response copywriters in the country. She's racked up dozens of successful direct mail and online controls, beating legendary copywriters such as Parris Lampropoulos and the late Jim Rutz—and becoming the first female copywriter to get a Boardroom control.

Kim writes winning copy and creates breakthrough marketing strategies for companies such as Soundview, Bottom Line, Green Valley Naturals, Healthy Directions, and many others, both in the United States, and from England to Germany to Singapore. She holds a Bachelor of Science in Mathematics and Statistics from Miami University in Ohio, and earned her MBA in Marketing from Loyola University, Maryland.

Kim credits her creative and analytical mind and marketing know-how for giving her a must-needed edge in today's increasingly competitive copywriting world—and wants to help others gain the same "marketing-savvy" advantage. That's why she writes a free weekly e-letter called *Copy Insiders*. You can get on Kim's list and find out more about learning from and working with her at www.KimSchwalm.com.

NOT-SO-SECRET
LESSON #10

RISE UP IN SPITE OF YOUR PAIN

∼

Adversity chose every single woman in this chapter. Assault, abuse, pain, divorce, death, addiction and more... none of the women asked for these challenges. None of them chose to suffer.

But in the face of life's adversities and challenges, you do have a choice. You can choose to give up, or you can choose to be resilient, to rise up again and again, as Andra Day sings in her anthem, 'Rise Up'.

> And I'll rise up
> I'll rise like the day
> I'll rise up
> I'll rise unafraid
> I'll rise up
> And I'll do it a thousand times again

Andra, a soul singer, wrote Rise Up as a prayer for herself during a difficult time. It went on to become an anthem for women facing difficult challenges everywhere.

Given that nine out of ten entrepreneurs fail, resilience or our ability to rise up, may be the single most important factor for success. It's what allows you to continue on in the face of gender and race bias and every other kind of bias you can imagine. It's what allows you to learn, grow, and transform your pain into something useful.

Each of the Titanides in this chapter chose to rise up, to thrive in spite of their challenges, in spite of their fear.

Karen is a thirty-two-year-old doctor in a prison when she is brutally assaulted by one of the inmates in her office. She tells her younger self, "Ask for help. Get mentors, coaching and people to help you when you don't know what to do or are uncomfortable. You may work in a prison, but that doesn't mean you need to imprison yourself."

One dark night decades ago when it's finally too much, Trudy jumps in her truck and runs from an abusive marriage. She tells her younger self, "The hard experiences either make you strong, or they break you, and you chose a long time ago that you're not a victim. Life has given you plenty of challenges, and while you don't get to choose your challenges, you do get to choose how to deal with them."

Rae watches her dream of becoming the first female Regimental Sergeant Major vanish as she's medically discharged from the Australian Army Pay Corps. She warns her younger self, "The pain and suffering of the next twelve years is going to test you beyond anything you've been through before. But surprisingly, the pain is a good thing. You're going to need the experience, coping skills and emotional resilience you use to manage that pain as you embark on your new mission as an entrepreneur..."

Cat's marriage ends and it becomes the most important turning point in her life. She reminds herself, "You are a phoenix, and you will overcome deadly fires to rise up from the ash. You are more powerful than you could have imagined, and you will rise as many times as life demands it. Trust yourself to do this."

When Angela loses the love of her life, she breaks open, but that breaking open becomes the stepping stone in her spiritual transformation. She tells her younger self, "You'll shed limiting beliefs and open yourself to trust in infinite possibilities—a world that your sheltered upbringing could never have allowed you to envision."

No one escapes life unscathed. There are going to be challenges and obstacles along the way, sometimes more painful than anyone should have to bear. But it's what you do when you face those moments that defines you. Don't give in, don't give up, chose to thrive. Rise up!

✿ 1 ✿

KAREN GEDNEY

∾

You may work in a prison, but that doesn't mean you need to imprison yourself.

DEAR KAREN AT THIRTY-TWO,

Tomorrow night you will have a thought, and will believe it to be the last thought of your life. The walls of your exam room will expand outward, then collapse inward in slow motion, and you will think, "Poor Clifton... I never even gave you a baby."

You won't be afraid as you hear the little pop-pop-pop sounds —shots fired by an assault team that kill Moth, the inmate who has taken you hostage. You will only be thinking of your husband, being left alone without you.

As this night ends, don't forget that he came to your mind first—not your sister, Joanie, not your parents. Don't miss a day without letting him know how much he means to you.

You will try to squash down and compartmentalize your anger at Moth for assaulting and raping you. That's going to cost

251

you, just as it always has when you have stuffed down intense emotions all throughout your life.

You did it in childhood because it was what you were taught to do, but you are not a child anymore. Go get some help and realize that you can experience anger without having to act on it. What is anger, really, but your response to a physical threat, an insult or idiocy?

When you go back to work on Monday, you will find that the prison did not expect you back yet. They will not have sealed the ragged hole in the wall of your office where they sledgehammered a hole to toss in the concussion grenade. They will not have scrubbed the tiles properly, and when you step on them, Moth's blood will come up between them.

Don't be surprised that the only compassion you feel in that prison comes from the inmates.

For a long time you will feel that the officers and staff don't care, because they won't say anything to you. Years later some of them will tell you how much it affected them and that they just didn't know what to say. You will realize that you yourself haven't fully recovered from PTSD until you ask how it affected other people besides yourself.

While none of your co-workers can even look you in the face, the inmates will look at you—really look at you—and tell you how sorry they are, how incredibly angry they are with Moth. Some of them will tell the guards they need treatments, just so they can bring you get-well cards that make you cry. Others will bring you tea throughout the day, write you poems, and risk getting written up by guards to look after you. They care about you, because you care about them.

I know it will be hard for you, but if there's any advice I can give you, it's this: the earlier you ask for help and get mentors, coaches and people to help you when you don't know what to do or are uncomfortable, the better off you will be.

You may work in a prison, but that doesn't mean you need to imprison yourself.

When you lock the door from the inside, you are the only one who has the key. But having someone on the other side to help pull it open makes it a lot easier to get out and do what you were meant to do.

You were meant to make the world a better and safer place. I know this is hard to believe, but when you finally stop practicing medicine your purpose will be more than just treating symptoms, whether it's in the medical world or the correctional world.

You will help shift where we as a society put our time, energy and resources. Not on the tail end of the problem, when the damage is already done, but at the beginning when it starts. Don't be afraid to ask for help, because you are going to need it.

Karen.

After three decades as a prison physician, upon release (retirement), KAREN GEDNEY is passionate about sharing her unique perspectives and interesting stories in her book, *30 Years Behind Bars*. As a national speaker and medical consultant speaker, she is focused on addressing the cause of problems versus. the symptoms, both in illnesses and in systems. She is dedicated to shifting the current prison paradigm from one of harm and recidivism to one of healing and reintegration. Another area she is particularly interested in is affecting positive behavior changes, optimal health, aging and mentoring at-risk youth. www.DiscoverDrG.com

2

RAE BRENT

~

If you aren't enjoying what you're creating, then create something different.

G'Day Rae,

You may think you're struggling right now, but you're about to hit a huge crossroad in your life, and hit it hard. Very soon, everything you believe in, all your dreams, and your goals will be forcefully removed from you without warning and without your consent.

You proudly aspired to being the first female Regimental Sergeant Major of the Royal Australian Army Pay Corps. And you were certainly on your way to making it happen. But after so many dedicated years of working your way up the ranks, you're about to be medically discharged from the Army.

It's going to be a massive adjustment at every level of your life. But try to remember to be proud of all you have achieved so far. Because the pain and suffering of the next twelve years is going to test you beyond anything you've been through before.

But surprisingly, the pain is a good thing. You're going to

need the experience, coping skills and emotional resilience you use to manage the pain as you embark on your new mission as a marketer, copywriter, entrepreneur and podcaster.

It's going to take you time to get your logical head around the idea that brain power is as important (if not more so) than physical power. Even though you are physically unable to contribute like you used to, you can and will contribute more to society with your thoughts and ideas than you could have ever imagined before.

(It's a good thing you're Tasmanian and have two heads... you're going to need the extra processing power for all the brilliant stuff you will create.)

So, here are my keys to live by. I hope you will take them onboard sooner than later:

1. THE BIGGEST AND BEST INVESTMENT YOU WILL EVER MAKE IS the one you make in yourself. You are totally worth it, so back yourself to the hilt!

2. DON'T GET CAUGHT UP IN EGO AND COMPETITION. LIVE your life according to your own inner guidance. Your dreams are more important than other people's, so never give away more of yourself than you are prepared to lose.

This also includes money. Live within your means, and if your means aren't enough to buy you what you want, upskill yourself and increase your means.

3. DO ALL THAT NEEDS TO BE DONE TODAY... AND NO MORE! There is a natural time and process to achieve your tasks. Make sure you can go to bed at night feeling like you have accomplished just what you needed to that day. You'll sleep better for it.

Life is a series of contrasts... sprints and marathons. Be prepared to push yourself when the need arises, but give yourself the gift of time... the time to rest, recover and recharge your batteries.

4. ABOVE ALL... HAVE FUN! YOU ARE THE ONE CREATING your life. So, if you aren't enjoying what you're creating, then create something different. Learn to lower your stress levels so you can live longer in your creative zone. Remember... you're not in the Army anymore. You get to decide what you do, who you do it with and when you do it!

BEFORE I GO, BECAUSE I KNOW YOU'RE THE 'MONEY WOMAN,' I have one last piece of advice that will help you. Always remember the "3 M's of Money"...

1. MANAGE THE MONEY YOU HAVE,

2. MAKE MORE MONEY, AND

3. MAXIMIZE HOW YOU ENJOY YOUR MONEY.

YOU'LL SHARE THIS AND OTHER MONEY WISDOM WITH YOUR audience and they'll love it. And they'll love you.

Your time in the Army was important to your life journey, but it doesn't define you. When you know this, you'll move powerfully forward towards your true purpose in life.

I KNOW you've got this! Now get out there and have a crack! Show the world how it's done!

Cheers,
Rae :)

RAE BRENT IS A BESTSELLING AUTHOR, PROPERTY Investor and Entrepreneur (Podcaster, Copywriter, Marketing Strategist and Mentor). She works behind the scenes as the "Secret Weapon" for her clients at her boutique marketing company, Camouflaged Marketing. Rae is passionate about helping business owners locate and capture the hidden money missing from their businesses.

She is the bestselling author of *The Money Mirror: How to Connect With Your Inner Self to Create Great Sustainable Wealth* and the creator of the *Discipline Your Dollars... To Get Out of Debt* online course.

YOU CAN FIND RAE ONLINE AT:
www.RaeBrent.com
www.BreakingThroughTheBS.com

❧ 3 ❧

CAT HARVEY

≈

The best thing you can do to heal your heart
is to forgive.

DEAR CATHY,

I know that the world seems dark right now, and that you've given up hope. Don't lose sight of the fact that you were created to be special, and to give your gifts to the world. Being married is only part of your story, and if you close your book now, you will miss the happy ending, and all the beautiful moments that come in between.

I know you can't accept it right now, but the end of your marriage will lead to the most important turning point of your life. At your lowest moment, everything will seem to fall away from you. And when you think you can't bear it anymore, you will find your spirit held and comforted by a higher love. That love will tell you how precious you are, and it will allow you to carry on.

Later on, you will realize that life is hard for every single person, not just you. Everybody is doing the best that they can—no one *wants* to do badly. Some people aren't capable of meeting your expectations. They just don't have the skills, understanding, or desire to do things differently. The best thing you can do to heal your heart is to forgive. By forgiving, you will make your own heart stronger. Don't be so hard on yourself, either. Take down that wall, and let yourself be loved.

You can't change other people. You can, however, take full control of yourself. Don't let other people have so much power over your sense of who you are. Stand up for yourself, and make your own decisions. You are a phoenix, and you will overcome deadly fires to rise up from the ash. You are more powerful than you could have imagined, and you will rise as many times as life demands it. Trust yourself to do this.

Don't take one minute for granted. The moments will pass whether you appreciate them or not. Your kids will become adults, and you will have grandchildren, and they will become adults quickly too. Be conscious of the time—it's true that you can't get it back.

Use the gifts you have been given. We have a responsibility to help each other, to lift each other up, and your positivity and humor can lift the spirits of everyone you come into contact with. Learn to give and receive help freely.

I'm not sure you can hear this now, but trust me on this. Have faith that things will work out exactly the way they're supposed to. You will get a second chance at love, and you will make a wonderful life. Hang in there.

Love you,

Cat

~

CAT HARVEY HAS LED A LIFE THAT HAS TAUGHT HER THE importance of reinventing herself. She has a wealth of work experience. She owned a service business for fifteen years, and then went on to own a retail business for ten years. After that, she did an eleven-year stint in corporate America. She has taken all of this business experience, and launched a career as a freelance writer.

Love is lovelier the second time around... Cat lives with her husband, Iain, just outside of Baltimore, Maryland. She has four children and two stepchildren. She enjoys spending time with them, and her seven grandchildren.

She embraces her long struggle with depression, because it's taught her many things she would not know otherwise. Working to overcome sadness has taught her to recognize and enjoy happiness. She is keenly aware that every road traveled as her younger self has led her to this point in her life, where she can be grateful for the blessings she has.

✻ 4 ✻

ANGELA TANGER

∼

You are enough. Stand in your own power. It will be infectious.

From my wisdom guide to my younger self...

Dearest Angela,

Let's get one thing straight. Your life will be filled with hills and valleys.

And you'll spend what seems like the majority of your time in the valley.

You see, the valleys are required training for your personal growth.

However, don't cower and hide in the valley too long...

Learn the lesson and move forward as gracefully and as quickly as possible.

One of your deepest valleys will be losing the love of your life. Your marriage will end, Andy will leave this world, and you, my dear, will be broken open...

But your breaking open will become the stepping stone in

your spiritual transformation. You'll meet lifelong friends in Al-Anon and they'll lead you step-by-step to a whole new path of self-discovery.

And yes, you'll love again, and again, and again...

Although you'll feel like a complete failure at relationships, I want you to know everyone takes a different life path. Your sister will marry her high-school sweetheart and build her life around motherhood. You, instead, will build your life around adventure.

Oh, the places you'll go—India, South Africa, France, Italy, Sedona, England, Ireland, Laos, Scotland, Wales, Alaska, Hawaii, Costa Rica. The people you'll meet. The memories you'll make. All priceless!

You'll shed limiting beliefs and open yourself to trust in infinite possibilities—a world that your sheltered upbringing could never have allowed you to envision.

So dear one, open your eyes, open your heart, and listen to wisdom speaking to you...

Be grateful for all of the missteps you'll take and how they'll propel you forward.

Flex your courage muscle! Be Brave. Be Bold. Be Authentic.

Just be YOU! You are enough. Stand in your own power. It will be infectious.

I love you, just as you are.

Your Wisdom Guide... aka "Angela"

P.S. No regrets, it's not over until it's over... you'll come to the end of this lifetime sliding in sideways, saying "Holy sh*t, what a ride!" You're time's not up yet, girl. Go for it NOW!

ANGELA TANGER HAS BEEN CHARTING HER OWN JOURNEY to health and wellness for the last twenty years. After seeing all three members of her immediate family—father, mother, and sister—battle cancer, Angela decided to become her own health advocate. Through a combination of traditional medicine and holistic healing, Angela has developed a healthy lifestyle that includes teaching yoga, eating a vegetarian diet, and practicing mindfulness in her daily life.

Angela is a direct-response copywriter and information marketer for alternative health. She is fiercely committed to helping wellness entrepreneurs uncover their personal transformation story, so they can relate to their ideal clients, and get their healing gifts out into the world.

Angela is the author of *Marketing Health & Wellness HER WAY: How to Connect & Engage with Women Buyers.*

You can connect with Angela at angela@angelatanger.com, or on Facebook and LinkedIn.

✹ 5 ✹

TRUDY BLACK

∼

The route to 'getting there' looks like a ball of yarn that a cat got hold of.

YOU DREAMED OF BECOMING A TRUCK DRIVER WHEN YOU were a child of ten, the day your dad brought that first truck home. You learned to drive it by the time you were twelve, puttering around the fields of your parents' dairy farm.

Every time your dad bought a new truck magazine, you would tear out the pictures of the fancy chrome trucks, all shiny and new, and post them on your bedroom walls—no rock bands or movie stars for you. The only other poster was a map of the United States. You were going to go there—everywhere—once you graduated high school, and you would go in a truck.

Looking back, the route to 'getting there' looks like a ball of yarn that a cat got hold of.

You found out you were pregnant in October of your senior year. Your parents, and his, said that you were supposed to get married. You were only interested in graduating... you've always had messed-up priorities.

When you found out your due date was in mid-July, you were

so relieved. You went along with everything else—getting married in January, graduating in June, turning eighteen on July 16th and having a C-section on the 19th.

And then you sucked it up. It was not the life you had envisioned for yourself. You were supporting your husband, and his drug and alcohol habits. Your parents didn't smoke, didn't drink, and you had never experienced anything like the abuse he started to heap on you.

You had no tools to deal with it, and so you stayed in the bed you had made.

Five years later you had another child, a little girl. Three months later she was taken by S.I.D.S., and even though her father blamed you, you decided you had to have another child. You were starting to realize that nothing is guaranteed, that you had to live for this moment, so you made a plan and eleven months later had another little girl.

Your marriage got gradually worse until there came a dark point late in 1994 when you couldn't stay married anymore—no matter what anyone thought. Not only were you fighting with your husband, but with your mother too. She insisted that people in our family just don't get divorced, and that things couldn't be that bad.

Despite everything she said, your parents had not raised you to be a doormat, so one night you jumped in that truck and ran. Ironically, you were safer trucking around all over the country than you were living in that house.

A year after getting a restraining order and filing for the divorce, you realized that you had to deal with everything that had happened: the pain was never going to go away until you processed what you had been through.

You had a lot of therapy, and figured out that it's easier to handle things as they happen, rather than letting things pile up until you're overwhelmed. You spent years building your self-esteem, and grew into a strong person who has no fear anymore.

You worked hard to have a relationship with your children,

which was almost a bigger challenge then gaining respect on the job.

You've driven over two million miles under your belt without accident, and you have worked very hard for that record. On the road you've seen the same lesson play out, again and again:

Deal with things that go wrong as they happen. Get through the moment of crisis, and if you must fall apart, do it later.

You've seen many accidents, and people react all kinds of ways—crying hysterically, or staring off into space on the side of the road, or putting up a barrier between the accident and themselves by taking photos to 'report' what happened—but you just get on with whatever needs to be done. You know you must be strong enough to get through the immediate situation, or there's going to be chaos far longer than necessary.

Sometimes you wonder if you really needed to go through all that suffering, if things could have been different. But the hard experiences either make you strong, or they break you, and you chose a long time ago that you're not a victim.

Without those experiences you never would have known what you're made of. Life has given you plenty of challenges, and while you don't get to choose your challenges, you do get to choose how to deal with them.

And now, at another crossroad, you get to choose again. There's not a lot of opportunity to grow—intellectually, spiritually or financially—driving a truck. Not even when you've reached the top of the industry, hauling fuel and chemicals.

You know that copywriting is the right road for you, and you've been travelling to Boot Camps and reading materials on how to do it since 2011. So get off the fence. Remember you aren't just 'good enough'—you're amazing. Step up, make a new career for yourself, and take your life back.

Trudy.

TRUDY BLACK HAS BEEN A PROFESSIONAL TRUCK DRIVER for over twenty years, and has been training and helping to educate other drivers for almost as long. She has been hauling hazardous materials for over five years, including petroleum and chemicals. She wants to be more involved in education and training of drivers to lower the fatality rate, which has drastically risen in the past couple years. She would also like to help to create training programs for the transportation industry, specifically geared towards safety, hazardous materials, regulations, and education in general.

To contact Trudy, email trudycblack@hotmail.com.

NOT-SO-SECRET
LESSON #11

NEVER STOP GROWING YOURSELF

~

When talking about personal growth, there's no entrepreneur who embodies this more than media queen, Oprah Winfrey. She says:

> "Life is about growth and change. When you are no longer doing that—that is your whisper; that is your whisper that you are supposed to do something else."

That whisper led Oprah from a small town in Mississippi to becoming the first African-American woman, and the youngest, to co-anchor the news in Nashville, Tennessee. That whisper led her from co-anchoring the news to launching the highest rated daytime talk show in American Television history and eighteen Emmy awards. That whisper led her to an academy award nomination for her breakout role in *The Color Purple*. And it led her to found her own production company, to launch her own magazine, and to build her own network.

Just like Oprah, the women in this chapter never stop

growing and they take advantage of every opportunity that comes their way.

Kira instructs her younger self, "Choose opportunities where you can take risks, fail, and grow. It might feel uncomfortable, but girl, discomfort is the only constant on the path to the type of success you want."

For Sarah, growth means chasing down the people who are already working the way she wants to work. She reminds herself, "You can spend years spinning your wheels, trying to figure out how to do this, or you can go find them, and learn how they are doing it. This is how you will build the life you want."

Carline started at $8 an hour in customer service but she knew she was built for bigger challenges. She held the company's financials hostage until the company President, Bob King, agreed to interview her for a position with the new health group. She got the position and that launched her career.

As she looks back, Carline honors her mother who gave her the opportunity to grow by uprooting her life in Haiti and starting over in America. Carline reminds her younger self, "Mom was right, as usual. She knew there was no excuse for you not to be successful. So, you uprooted your own life and started a new chapter as a freelance copywriter. And now you get to see your own children growing every day through different stages of life."

Susan sacrificed her own growth for her husband for twelve years until she finally realized that when you hide your gifts, you suppress your true self and you slight the Creator. She urges her younger self, "Your talents are for the benefit of others, and your business is for the benefit of the world. When you avoid doing what you must do, you are withholding something the world deeply needs." Never negate yourself or your own growth!

Molly's boss literally pushes her onto the stage at the 2016 Traffic & Conversion Summit in front of two thousand people. And that's when she suddenly sees what her boss already knew, that she was exactly where she needed to be. And that is when

Molly begins to see herself as a speaker and teacher and creator. So in that moment she urges her younger self, "Trust yourself. Trust the universe. Don't ignore the opportunities that come your way and don't put yourself in a box."

Oprah is clear that her success is not about luck, it's about taking advantage of every opportunity for growth. "I believe luck is preparation meeting opportunity. If you hadn't been prepared when the opportunity came along, you wouldn't have been lucky."

Your job is to prepare yourself. So that when a new opportunity for growth opens up, you are ready for success.

SUSAN BERKLEY

~

If you put off your life's purpose until the eleventh hour, there will come a point of no return.

DEAR SUSAN,

You were born with business in your blood. Your grandfather started Archie Comics in 1941, and your father went into the family business before you were born.

Because you loved rock and roll, it never occured to you to join the family business, so you worked in radio for fifteen years. You started at the college radio station, then moved to Florida to host an afternoon drive show. After a while you came back to New York City, and then you met the Brazilian rockstar.

THE BRAZILIANS

You didn't even know where Brazil was, but Sérgio was *hot*, and you eloped to Rio de Janeiro with him. You were twenty-six and lived in Rio for six months, learned to speak Portuguese, and when you came back to NYC together, he started suffering from panic attacks. You found an ad from Dr. Keppe, a Brazilian psychoanalyst who had just opened a clinic a block from your apartment. You made an appointment for Sérgio and then another for your own anxiety.

Sérgio didn't like the therapy. He left and you split up (which was just as well, because Latin rock stars are great fun, but *not* marriageable material).

Dr. Keppe, on the other hand, will be part of your life from now on. You will study his work for the next thirty years and it will inform everything you do. You will study and teach at The Keppe-Pacheco College of Trilogical Studies in Sao Paulo Brazil for six weeks each year to continue your growth. You become a certified instructor of Keppe's unique therapeutic methodology and use it to help your clients overcome anxiety and speak with confidence.

THE MAN WITH THE JAG

When you moved back to NYC, you landed a job as the traffic reporter for the Howard Stern Show. That had the intended effect of making you famous, but you were hardly making any money, so you decided that you would get into voice-over work.

You quit radio and assumed the world would beat a path to your door in order to hire you—you were famous, after all—but you launched to crickets. The work was sporadic at best, and after one job, you saw another voice-over actor getting into a Jaguar sedan while you were fishing in your pocket for subway change.

You thought to yourself, *there's something wrong with this picture.* A crazy idea flashed into your head, and Susan, that idea changed your life.

You raced across the parking lot and begged that man to take to you to lunch. He agreed, and over your meal you asked what he was doing that you were not. He just said, "When I'm not working, I'm marketing myself."

At that moment, a lightbulb went off in your head. You realized you could struggle trying to audition just a little bit better than anybody else, but you knew actors have very little control over who gets picked. If you learned all about sales and marketing, on the other hand, you would have total control over your work.

You heard that Jay Abraham was running a marketing seminar for $5000, which was *crazy* money for you at the time, but you found one credit card that wasn't tapped out and put that seminar on it. It was totally worth it—you learned everything you needed to get started. Jay taught you all about direct marketing, about the customer and the three ways to grow a business... and you were hooked.

THE VILLAGE VOICE

After Jay's seminar you decided to start running workshops teaching people how to get into voice-over work. You had no clue what you were doing, You had never run a workshop before, but you had nothing to lose so you just took an ad out in the back of the Village Voice among all the singles ads that said *"Make money with your voice!"*

People started signing up in droves, and you learned very quickly how to make it work. You went to a women's business course at the Fashion Institute of Technology, which was packed with great speakers, you connected yourself with consultants, and by God did you read! You bought as many books as you could, devouring all the expertise people had put into writing about marketing and sales.

You opened a school, training people in voice-over, and before long you had tons of students. Then your own voice-over work took off as well, and in 1990 you opened The Great Voice Company in NYC. Your gift for business and leadership bloomed—you hired employees, had a recording studio, you were training people, running seminars, and everything was going incredibly well.

THE SUBURBS AND THE SUPPRESSION

You loved living in NYC. When The Great Voice Company took off, everyone in the city knew who you were and you had hundreds of people coming through your classes.

Then you met a new guy and got married. It was not a good choice.

He became very jealous of your success and tried to convince you to close the business and move out into the suburbs. He had all these big ideas about what we were going to do, and you did as he asked.

You closed your business and moved to the suburbs, and you quickly got very sick. You developed an autoimmune disease.

We are all given gifts by God but when we hide those gifts and suppress who we truly are, we slight our Creator. By doing so, we unconsciously attempt to negate ourselves, an impossibility, but nevertheless, we keep trying. The tension and internal discord have to go somewhere, and in your case, it turned your body against itself.

You'll learn in time that this suppression of self is a very common thing among women. They hold themselves back, often using their guy as an excuse, and you realized that this had been your hidden intention—to stop your own success.

Men are not the enemy here, and women are not victims. Dr Keppe helped you understand that all of us have something in our unconscious minds that rejects goodness and displaces the blame for our unhappiness onto somebody else.

You chose a marriage partner who wasn't a good fit for you, because your unconscious intention was against yourself and your own growth. You know now that you can't blame everything on him, because you *chose* him to do something that you unconsciously wanted to do to yourself.

That marriage lasted twelve years, and when it finally ended it created a huge turning point for you. Toward the end, you reopened the business, and after the divorce you picked yourself up and focused on regrowing it. It quickly began to thrive, and as you started to step into your gifts again, your autoimmune disease was healed.

THE GIFTS

Your unique ability is helping others clarify their message so they can deeply connect with their audience and stop getting in their own way in their leadership and sales and marketing presentations.

Remember that your talents are for the benefit of others, and your business is for the benefit of the world. On those days where you procrastinate, think about that. If you put off your life's purpose until the eleventh hour, there will come a point of no return and deep regret as you get older. When you avoid doing what you must do, you are withholding something the world deeply needs.

So do it for humanity, and do it for yourself! The greatest thing in the world is to be independent, and that is the great gift you receive in return for sharing yours.

Go for it, girl.

All my love,

Susan.

∾

SUSAN BERKLEY IS THE FOUNDER OF THE GREAT VOICE Company and www.greatvoice.com. She is the author of *Speak To Influence: How To Unlock The Hidden Power Of Your Voice* and *The Persuasion Code*. A top voice-over artist, she is the signature voice of Citibank and one of the most listened-to voices in America. The audio production division of The Great Voice Company provides professional voice talent recording services in all languages for companies and marketers world-wide.

After three decades of successfully coaching and mentoring thousands of aspiring voice-over artists in her unique Mic To Money™ method at www.mictomoney.com, Susan came to understand that marketers and business leaders are missing a huge growth opportunity when they fail to fully optimize their on-line and live presentations with vocal influence and authentic speaking techniques. However, many professionals avoid the opportunity to influence, sell and lead through speaking and video messages because of the anxiety they feel.

In this vein, Susan has transformed her business with a professional division at speaktoinfluence.com, offering live and online speaking and voice mastery workshops for growth-focused business owners and sales and customer service organizations. Susan believes that authentic speaking should be an act of affection, not an exercise in forced precision or manipulation. True charisma is fed by an honest desire to be of service, not by dazzlingly complex Powerpoint ® presentations, fist pumps or phony energy-enhancing exercises.

Speak To Influence is a uniquely effective program because it is based on Dr Keppe's proven therapeutic methodology and Susan's trademarked Vocal Influence techniques. It succeeds where other speaking programs fail, helping participants speak confidently and comfortably with clarity, energy and authenticity.

For more information click or call: www.speaktoinfluence.com or The Great Voice Company at 800-333-8108.

❧ 2 ❧

KIRA HUG

~

Discomfort is the only constant on the path to the type of success you want.

LOYALTY IS A LAIR, K-DAWG...

And hidden deep within that cave of devotion, you'll find Fear, curled up in the fetal position with a slew of Reese's peanut butter cup wrappers nearby.

Hiding from possibility, growth, and your purpose.

You may trick yourself into thinking you're such a loyal person—like, so loyal you deserve a badge or something—but maybe you're not actually that loyal.

Maybe your loyalty is just a mask... maybe it's just protecting your fear of the unknown.

Your parents' generation believed that being loyal to a career, corporation, and path would lead to financial success, peace of mind, and a safe future (hello, retirement!).

But what if they were duped?

Remember when you were in college and your dad lost a significant portion of his income and retirement, because the company he was loyal to for decades fell into bankruptcy? Yeah, that sucked.

Loyalty didn't stand a chance, and if you want to achieve success in today's marketplace, you need to guide yourself through the twists and turns. You need to know when to zig, when to zag, and when to zug (and zugging is always fun!).

Choose opportunities where you can take risks, fail, and grow. It might feel uncomfortable, but girl, discomfort is the only constant on the path to the type of success you want.

NO ONE can tell you when you need to move from job A... to job B... to job Z. Trust your intuition, pursue your interests, and chase down the next challenge, like a bulldog.

Oh, and good news! As it turns out, challenges light you up. That may mean you only stay at your cushy job at that nonprofit for two years, even though the benefits are awesome. Even though you have your own office. Even though you respect your colleagues and feel one hundred percent autonomous.

But, are you willing to sacrifice your future business, creative freedom, and affluence for safety? Nah.

Here's a fun fact: You never would have pursued your dream of working for a startup, and you never would have started your own business, if you had stayed in your air-conditioned office.

K-HUG, you need to trust your gut when it tells you, *"Hey girl, time to move on!"* because—get this—NO ONE ELSE WILL TELL YOU! You're the only one who's got the directions folded neatly in your back pocket.

Now, I'm not telling you to be unreliable, irresponsible, or a flaky flakester. I am saying this: set clear intentions before you step into a new role.

And ask yourself a few questions:

What do I hope to achieve?

How will I know when I've accomplished that goal?

How long do I estimate it will take me?

Once you know roughly how long it will take you to accomplish your goal(s) for that particular position, pencil it in on the calendar.

And when you hit that milestone, whether it's two years later or five years later...

Take time to assess where you stand, what you've accomplished, and what growth opportunities remain.

If you've hit a plateau, it's time to go. Maybe that means choosing a new position in a new department. Maybe that means leaving a company to join another. Maybe it's a more radical change, and you pursue a new venture altogether, like entrepreneurship. Or, maybe it means something else you'd never expect.

Stay open to all opportunities that await. Stay open, stay open, stay open.

Question your loyalty to ideas, careers, and companies often.

And save your loyalty for loved ones, values, and your ambition.

If you do that, my old friend, you'll lead a happy life.

IN A PREVIOUS LIFE, KIRA HUG WAS AN ART MAJOR (YEP) ended up working with global brands like Estee Lauder Companies. She also led the marketing team for startups like ActionableBooks.com and global health nonprofits (*what up, glaucoma and breastfeeding*).

Today, Kira calls herself a Copy Chef (she likes to dress like a chef, even though you'll rarely find her in a kitchen). Kira leads a team of multiple copywriters in a flex micro-agency focused on personality-driven launch copy for courses and membership programs. Basically, she helps her clients package and sell their unique brand of 'weird.'

Kira also co-hosts *The Copywriter Club* podcast with Rob Marsh, where she interviews the most forward-thinking copywriters about their processes, routines, structure, and best advice.

She also runs 'The Copywriter Think Tank', a high-level mastermind for copywriters, content writers and strategists. And they lead 'The Copywriter Underground', a fast-growing paid membership focused on helping copywriters master their copywriting, business skills, and mindset.

When Kira's not in Type-A, NYC workaholic mode, she's running at Prospect Park, watching her fave movie for the zillionth time (*she will find you, Last of the Mohicans!*), or attempting to play the violin with her daughter (*it's their new thing, don't judge*).

Kira currently lives in Brooklyn with her husband and two kids... but she's relocating to Washington, DC soon.

3

SARAH PETTY

~

Someone else has already figured out how to do this.

Dear Sarah,

When you finally got pregnant with your twins in 2000, you had no idea you would be spending eighteen of the next thirty-three weeks in hospital or on bedrest. You had no idea how hard that pregnancy was going to be, but you also had no idea what a transformative time that was going to be for you.

You had to let go of the marketing job you loved, but you found yourself with time to think about what kind of parent you wanted to be. You found yourself thinking about your own parents.

When you were in college, your parents had come to every volleyball tournament you played out of state. They weren't wealthy, by any means—your dad was an entrepreneur, and taught at a community college—but they saved, they shopped flights, they took transfers and did whatever they had to in order to be there for you.

A lot of your teammates were lucky if their parents made it

to one game in an entire season. It was terrible! You wanted to call child protective services because they were being so neglected! Of course, you only realized later on how hard it is for parents to show up like that, but your parents built their whole life around being able to be there for you. Your dad worked nights and odd weekends, and didn't teach Fridays at the community college so he could leave whenever he needed to.

Lying there on bedrest, you knew that was the kind of parent you wanted to be. You knew you wanted to be able to go to the 10am school programs when the kids were little, you wanted to be able to pick them up from school every day, and you wanted to see them actually grow up day to day.

You had been doing photography for fun, and had a legal pad of people who said they would wait until you had the babies to have you do pictures for them. So after the twins were born you decided you weren't going back to the agency and that you were going to start your own business, using this 'family first' filter.

Since you weren't a trained photographer, you had a lot of insecurities and doubts when you got started. Even though you had an undergraduate degree in business, and an MBA, you had no idea how to price for your business and how to sell—selling your own work is not what they teach you in business school.

Entrepreneurship is a whole different game, and you made every mistake in the book. You were massively underpriced, you didn't have a sales system of any kind, you were giving away proofs and extra services for free and working yourself to death.

One day, looking at your checkbook and wondering how on earth you were still so short on money when you were working so hard, you realized that someone else had already figured out how to do this. *You could spend years spinning your wheels, trying to figure out how to do this, or you could go find them, and learn how they are doing it.*

Sarah, start looking for the people who are working like you want to work—the people with flexible schedules, pipelines full of prospects, and full control over their work and time. Save your money, call them up, fly to wherever they are in the country, and learn from them. This is how you will build the life you want.

When you start implementing the things you learn from those people, your photography business will turn around and become profitable quickly. So quickly, in fact, that you'll start being asked to speak at industry events and teach your processes. Soon the demand for your second business, Joy of Marketing, will emerge, and eventually you'll be teaching photographers around the world how to do what you did.

Most businesses compete with cheap, but photographers compete with free. Everyone has a digital camera and a smartphone, so you will write a book called *Worth Every Penny: How to Build a Business That Thrills Your Customers & Still Charge What You're Worth*. You know now that it's not about price—people aren't looking for the cheapest provider. Price will sometimes be the issue, but you know that people are looking for great experiences with their service providers, and you teach that every chance you get.

This gift your parents gave you—being able to choose your own filter, and being focused on always finding a solution—keeps you growing constantly. You always have a coach, you're always investing in education for yourself and your team, and you are always able to look at big decisions with clarity. You still find the people who have something you want and go learn from them.

And through it all, you get to invest in your family first. You get to go to the recitals and games and ceremonies, because you created your own filters and chose what was right for you. You've built the life you want, and you love it, because you knew your own worth and that you only had to choose what was right for you.

Sarah.

~

SARAH PETTY IS A HIGHLY-ACCLAIMED MARKETING speaker, best-selling marketing author of *Worth Every Penny: Build a Business that Thrills Your Customers and Still Charge What You're Worth*, MBA and photography marketing teacher who has inspired thousands of boutique photography business owners to use beautiful marketing to take their business to the next level. Her expertise is based on over twenty years helping build the Coca-Cola brand, meeting the marketing goals of a top regional advertising agency's clients and building her own successful Springfield, Illinois boutique photography studio. This studio, Sarah Petty Photography, was named one of the most profitable in the country within just five years in business. Sarah has mastered the science of marketing and the art of making it simple, actionable, and, yes, fun!

❦ 4 ❦

MOLLY PITTMAN

~

Surround yourself with the people who lift you,
and remember, always, to trust yourself

"Hey, Molly—I know we didn't talk about this yet, but we need you to go on the main stage next week to talk about how you've been running our Facebook ads."

YOUR BOSS WAS LOOKING AT YOU WITH THAT INNOCENT LOOK on his face, like it was no big deal he had just told you that in four days, you would be speaking to over two thousand people, at one of the biggest marketing events in the world, with no warning and no stage experience.

You had been hired as an intern at Digital Marketer, a highly successful online marketing agency, three years ago, soon after college. You had been promoted, and promoted, and now, at twenty-six, you were the VP of Marketing for the whole company.

But this was a curveball you had not seen coming, and it made you so nervous that you made yourself sick for the whole weekend. You turned yourself inside out worrying that you were going to fail, analyzing and re-analyzing every way the session could go wrong. You had never felt less ready for anything.

But when you stepped out onto that stage at the 2016 Traffic & Conversion Summit, you realized that you were *exactly* where you needed to be.

You suddenly saw what your boss saw—that you do this stuff successfully every day, that you know how to get people to pay attention, and most importantly, that you love helping people.

Until that moment, you would never have thought of yourself as a speaker or teacher, but sharing how people could grow their businesses—which would let them send their kids to college, hire people in their communities, change their local economies —aligned you with your purpose in life.

That was when you discovered how much meaning there could be in work, and how much fun.

As you kept speaking more, creating courses to teach people online, building a podcast, meeting one-on-one with entrepreneurs and other marketers, you realized that this is what you're here for. You're great at marketing, but your real purpose is to teach other people how to do it.

And when you finally start your own agency, you will use those skills to build a community of businesspeople around you who want to change the world.

One of those businesspeople, Colleen Taylor, will tell you soon after you start working together that while she would love her kids to be great marketers, she really just wants them to be emotionally responsible and to know how to deal with other people.

Because that's what life—and marketing—is about: connecting deeply with other people, and making your best effort to interact in a positive way.

Marketing can, and has, changed the world, and so as you build your agency, you will choose your clients very carefully. You will select people with whom you have fun and camaraderie, but more importantly, you will select people who really believe in the purpose of their work and who want to use their influence for good.

You know that marketing has huge inherent power, and you believe deeply that marketers and businesspeople have a huge social responsibility—that how we deploy our words, emotions and influence has to have a positive influence on the people we are interacting with.

As you start facilitating this online life for so many entrepreneurs, you will want to make sure that you do what's best for everyone. This is hard—different people have different ideas of what that means—and it's not always the thing that makes the most money. But it's okay. When you come from a place of wanting to get the best result for everyone involved, things will work out.

So Molly, trust yourself. Trust the universe. Don't ignore the opportunities that come your way, and don't put yourself in a box. Remember that when you answered that ad for the internship, you could never have imagined where you would be just a few years later. You can't plan your life down to the last detail, and even if you do, it won't make you happy.

Focus on finding fulfilment and joy. Let your work be fun. Surround yourself with the people who lift you and others, and remember, always, to trust yourself.

Love and gratitude,

Molly.

～

MOLLY PITTMAN IS A DIGITAL MARKETING EXPERT AND educator. She has certified thousands of marketers in paid traffic and customer acquisition, and is a co-host of the Perpetual

Traffic Podcast, which has grown to over four million downloads in three years.

She is the cofounder of www.teamtraffic.com, www.trainmytrafficperson.com, and www.digitalstrategy-bootcamps.com providing education and coaching to help media buyers get better results with paid traffic. Molly started her career as an intern at DigitalMarketer.com in 2012, excelling to VP of Marketing in 2014, a position she held until 2017 when she left to start her own consulting agency. At DigitalMarketer, Molly personally spent $14+ million on paid traffic channels like Facebook, Google, and Twitter while maintaining a positive return on investment. She lives in Colorado.

❧ 5 ❧

CARLINE ANGLADE-COLE

❧

Own your decisions.

HIYA CARLINE,

Remember all the stories your mom used to tell you about Haiti? How hard life was, the poverty. She wanted better for you and your sister When she married Gerry, it took them two years to save up enough money and find a decent place to live so you and Viv could come to America.

Remember all the jobs she used to juggle? Maid, cashier, selling Avon. She couldn't even really speak English, so you went knocking on the doors as the Avon lady! At least she gave you a piece of her commission.

Remember all the times your mom told you there was no excuse not to be successful in America?

It's easy to see where you got your work ethic, and the big dreams you had for building a successful career. But you also wanted a big family.

So when the kids were still small and you stumbled on an ad for a marketing company that was just fifteen minutes away from your house—and you saw 'flexible schedule' advertised—you knew you had to follow up on it.

Phillips Publishing was a young, entrepreneurial direct marketing company. The people were awesome, and Tom Phillips encouraged all his employees to bring ideas to the table. You started in the customer service department, making $8 an hour answering phones. But it wasn't long before you moved up and took on new challenges—keeping your part-time, flexible-hour schedule.

When you heard a new division was being created for the health market, you knew you had to get in on that. Even though you didn't know anything about marketing, you knew you could learn fast. It was such a cool opportunity, wasn't it? You couldn't have known that it would change your life in so many ways.

Remember how you held the company's financials—known affectionately as the green sheet—for ransom until Bob King agreed to interview you? That was *risky*. He could have fired you right there on the spot. And rightfully so—he was the Vice President of the Company! But he didn't. Instead he gave you an appointment for an interview. Phew!

Remember that interview? How could you forget?! The green-and-blue trimmed suit you spent days sewing was ruined because you were sweating so much. You've never had another interview like that in your entire career! Bob grilled you for two and a half hours on a Friday afternoon, and you walked out of that interview thinking you blew it. You were so bummed the entire weekend.

But on Monday morning, Marshall Hamilton called and said, "I don't know what you said to Bob but he said to get you on this team. So welcome to the team!"

You became the Assistant Marketing Manager for the fledgling health group.

It was hard the first year. Nothing worked. It was just you and Marshall on the marketing team, and your first few launches bombed. It wasn't until the launch of *Health & Healing* that the group got any respect.

And remember who wrote that launch copy? Yep—Clayton Makepeace. Can you believe you actually got to work and spend time with Clayton Makepeace? Never in your wildest dreams did you think he would be your mentor and one of your oldest business friends.

When Wendy joined your team, *Health & Healing* became unstoppable! Your career grew by leaps and bounds. You and Wendy worked like crazy—but it was worth it. Wendy and Clayton eventually got married and you kept working at Phillips for twelve years. Along the way, you uncovered you had a knack for this thing called 'copywriting'.

So you and Mick talked it over, prayed about it and then worked out a plan. It was time to take the plunge and try this freelance copywriting thing. Man oh man were you scared!

It seems like yesterday but twenty years have passed. The kids are grown. You still love your husband. You have four awesome grandsons. You've done lots of volunteer work with your congregation. You've had amazing travel opportunities.

You kept your priorities straight, and put your family and spiritual goals first and then your career. You have your husband to thank for that—he's the real secret to your success and happiness.

And you've never regretted that decision to become a freelance copywriter. Not once. Because even if the money hadn't been phenomenal, the freedom you had as a freelancer would have made it all worthwhile.

So your mom was right, as usual. She gave you the opportunity by uprooting her life and starting a new one in America. She knew there was no excuse for you to not be successful—and now you see your own kids, and it's like deja vu!

You uprooted your life, and started a new chapter, and now you get to see your younger self growing every day through different stages in life, like your mom got to see you, Viv and your baby brother Greg growing. You can relate to what your kids are experiencing because it happened to you. They have a lot to still learn and fortunately, you're not shy about giving advice.

So here's what you want your younger selves to know...

FOR THE YOUNG MOTHER:

Enjoy the restless nights with the kids waking up at all hours. That might sound crazy, since it seems hard right now. But this is the easy part. Right now you know where they are! The hard part comes when they're teenagers and you don't know where they are or what they're doing. You'll wish for these nights again!

So let them all get in the bed with you, whenever they want. It's crowded with six pairs of legs in one bed, but cherish it. You've made the decision to be a parent, so own that decision. Be in the moment and in every experience—don't wish it away, or dream about them going off to school already. It will happen way faster than you would ever want.

You can have it all, but you can't have it all at the same time, so make your plan and stick with it. You can make changes to the plan but be true to it. If you're going to be a stay-at-home mom, stay at home and raise your kids the best way you know how. If you are going to be a working mom, be the best working mom possible. Do the best you can with whatever decision you make.

You'll eventually see that *it's not fair* is a totally accurate assessment of child-rearing. Every one of your kids' personalities are completely different—so it's impossible to be 'fair.' Just do what you need to in order to bring out the best in each one as individuals. They'll love you for it... but maybe not until they have kids of their own!

FOR THE YOUNG ADVENTURER:

Keep sticking to your guns. Don't settle. You're teased by your friends for having higher standards than them... like waiting for your knight in shining armor is a bad thing!

Appreciate and respect the path your friends have taken—but don't compare your journey with theirs. It's a waste of energy.

Stop projecting where you think you should be, or what you should be doing, or what people are thinking about you. Just be you, true to who you are.

Don't wear yourself out looking at every person who comes by, wondering if they're 'the one'—let someone appear that's worthy! It's okay. You've got time. You might feel like you've been waiting so long, but there's no rush. He'll show up and you'll be glad you waited when it happens.

And in the meantime, enjoy your life!

Keep travelling, exploring new places and living in cities you love. Keep on building up your career and business, and own where you are at right now. Some of your friends are looking at you like you have the best life ever!

FOR THE ONE STRUGGLING:

When you're in flux, understand that mistakes help you grow. It's your life, your path, and you have to come to understand how decisions are going to affect you. If someone else steps in to save you, it will handicap you. All this struggle and pain will help you get to the next level and to become the person you're supposed to be.

There's a story about a little girl who found an egg that had fallen out of a nest. She took the egg home to care for it, and after a few days, she heard some noise inside the egg as the baby bird started to try to get out. Every day, she would watch the egg, hear the pecks, and she grew impatient. she decided to speed things up by helping to break the shell. She did and the bird came out.

But the bird looked frail and weak, and never learned how to properly fly. What the little girl didn't realize was that the struggle of trying to break the shell was a good thing. It was preparing the bird for life on the outside, and would have helped the bird grow strong. By 'helping', the little girl handicapped the bird for life.

It's hard to watch a struggle like this unfolding from the outside. When you're in the struggle, you want someone to come and break you out, and simultaneously for everyone to leave you alone. When you're seeing the struggle, all you want to do is hug and heal and help, but you can't—that would be breaking the shell too soon.

Ultimately, all you can do is hope that attitude and independence are channeled in positive ways. Watch. Pray. Wait. Pray. Breathe. Pray. Give space as needed... oh, and PRAY!

FOR THE STUBBORN ONE:

Free will and freedom are very different. You have the free will to choose but you don't have the freedom to change the rules—especially rules of God. So, yes, you have the free will to climb a ten-story building and jump out of the window. You may even have the opportunity to make a phone call—and even enjoy the descent. But you will fall and hit rock bottom. It's an unbreakable rule.

When you're stubborn, you make it even more difficult on yourself.

That stubborn streak is definitely inherited from both sides of your family. Stubbornness allowed you to ride a bike without training wheels at two years old. You would not give up no matter how many times you fell off. Stubbornness allowed you to win the big prize at the carnival. The determination in your eyes as you tried to make the basketball shot was eerie. But you did it.

But when stubbornness turns to haughtiness—it's a different animal. Be careful of that. It's not who you are, but it looks like it from other people's perspective. Channel stubbornness into determination to do the right thing and you will succeed. Realize that you are part of a family and your role will never be filled by anyone else. Respect that privilege and honor and find your way back home.

CARLINE ANGLADE-COLE SPECIALIZES IN CREATING home-run copy to launch new products, revive struggling product lines, and help clients to maximize their revenues. She still wakes up every morning shocked and happy that she's found a job that pays her so well for doing something she loves!

After twelve years in the direct mail industry working at Phillips Publishing Inc. (now Healthy Directions), Carline ventured out on her own and launched Cole Marketing Solutions, Inc.

When she began her copywriting freelance career in 1999—her goal was simple: Make a decent income and have the flexibility and time to raise her four kids with her firefighter husband, Mickey.

Along the way, she managed to create multi-year controls for leading clients in the health industry, consulted and helped international clients break into the American health market, and got a shot at launching Oprah's *O Magazine* in the direct mail arena.

Thanks to the amazing writer's life, Carline and her family have traveled around the world to countries like Japan, Sri Lanka, Guatemala, Australia, New Zealand, South Africa, Mexico, the Caribbean, Madagascar, Kenya, Korea and Thailand —just to name a few.

For more about Carline, visit: www.carlinecole.com

NOT-SO-SECRET
LESSON #12

LEAD LIKE THE WOMAN YOU ARE

~

When Sheryl Sandberg wrote *Lean In* in 2013, she was addressing the crisis in leadership in the executive suite. She pointed out the gap between men and women in the professional world. Women were not promoted as often as men. Women were paid less than their male colleagues for the same job. And women were more likely than men to cut back or drop out of the workforce all together after having children. In her legendary TED talk, Sandberg encouraged women to address the gender gap by leaning in and actively pursuing leadership roles in corporate America.

Now, new research from the Lean In organization and McKinsey reveals that more women are stepping up and asking, but they are still eighteen percent *less* likely to be promoted than their male colleagues. The gender pay gap is even worse for women of color, who earn even less than white women and dramatically less than white men. And corporate America still remains largely white and male. Women leaned in, but they didn't get the results they hoped for.

Since Sandberg's book was published, #MeToo has put the

fear of God into the mostly white male leadership, with the unexpected backlash that men are now afraid to mentor women. A new survey from Lean In finds that half of all male managers are nervous about working alone or closely with a woman.

That's why today more than ever, it's on women to step up and lead. The backlash means that women at all levels of business need to actively mentor other women. We need to hold the door open for the next woman in line behind us. And we must use our collective influence to change the corporate culture for *all* women, not just white middle and upper class women.

Women bring unique skills to the workplace and corporations succeed better when there is balanced leadership. As the Titanides in this chapter demonstrate, you do *not* have to become a man in order to lead. You can lead like a woman.

Karri is 37-years-old before she finally realizes she doesn't need a penis to lead. She tells her younger self, "You don't need a penis to swing around or to whip out and measure to manage a team. Give your team something to be proud of. Something to own. Hand them a piece of the business to run that allows their strengths to shine." Remember, you don't have to lead like a man. You can lead like *you* and still get the raises, the praises, and the promotions.

Mary too learns that you don't need a penis to lead. After years of watching women be silenced in a culture made by men, for men, she decides to create a new kind of writing community —one that is led by women, for women—to nurture and celebrate their individual voices. She creates a school where women can find their voices, speak their truths and tell their stories in a world in which they were often silenced.

She tells her younger self, "Remember that everyone is afraid and everyone is vulnerable. Remember, too, that fear and vulnerability can be transformed into courage and compassion when there is a safe container to facilitate that transformation." You must create the container that allows transformational change to occur.

For Tepsii, the courage to lead is forged in her childhood growing up in South Africa. People died. People went to prison, lost all their possessions, and were excommunicated from their communities. Her family and friends suffered, a lot, to create change in the world.

Tepsii encourages her younger self, "Not seeing other people that look like you doesn't mean there's not space for you—it means that you get to create that space and become that role model for yourself, and for others. Choose to show up, and to use the voice you've cultivated to speak on behalf of those who don't yet have their own voices. Remember, when you're afraid, when you think you're just a breeder who will never amount to anything, show up anyway."

Jenny Thompson was ten years old when she learned to lead. Her parents divorced, her mother had a breakdown, and in the months that followed Jenny discovered that nobody was in charge in her home anymore. So she learned to get by, to get herself to school on time and to cover for her rebellious older sister. It wasn't easy. But those years shaped Jenny and made her the leader she is today.

She tells her younger self, "When things are uncertain, you know how to step into the breach. Leadership is about steering that ship whether the seas are calm or stormy or full of sharks, and you have built the fundamental skills throughout your life to do that wherever you find yourself." Remember, someone always has to be in charge.

For Annie, the path to becoming a leader was also forged in difficulty. When she takes over the family business in her twenties, she is convinced that she knows more than everyone else, that there is nothing left for her to learn having grown up in the business and studied economics and worked in big finance. And it's her arrogance that teaches her the hard lessons of leadership.

It isn't until the CFO storms out of her office calling her a "bitch in an ivory tower," that Annie finally learns to listen. She tells her younger self, "Through your own suffering, you will learn to appreciate how we all suffer. And this discovery will lead you to the biggest source of strength in your life: compassion. Compassion for yourself and others will become your 'magic wand' that allows you to heal deep hurts and turn pain into love." Remember, you must learn to listen to the people you are leading if you want to grow.

Like Annie, Sarah takes over the leadership of her dad's company. Her dad was a visionary and a genius in his day, but that day is gone. Sarah realizes that in order to lead, she must let go of the past. She tells her younger self, "Don't be afraid to do things differently, to create a new legacy. If you don't you will fail." Remember that, "Because we've always done it that way" won't fly anymore. Everything must be up for review, no matter how big or small.

On the fifth anniversary of *Lean In*'s publication, Sandberg recently told Bloomberg Businessweek, "We had a lot of work to do then, and we have a lot of work to do now." No matter where you are at in your career or how far up you are on the corporate ladder or how successful you are as an entrepreneur, you have something to offer another woman. The only way the culture will change is if we all work together to actively change it. It's time to step up and lead like the woman you are.

1

KERRI SHANNON

~

You don't have to 'lead like a man.'

DEAR KERRI:

At age thirty-seven, you don't have a penis. And you have no plans to get one.

But even so, you manage a team of twenty.

And I just know you're wondering, *"How did I ever get to be in charge of a team if I don't have a penis? A penis to swing around, to whip out and see who is most important compared to other managers?"*

It's okay. You don't need anything to come out of your pants for people to know you're a leader. The two things are unrelated.

Now, you might be thinking, *"But... how did I get people to fear me? Did I yell, or insult them, or slam my fists on their desks?"*

It's okay. You don't need—or want—your employees to fear you, or your temper.

You see, when your employees don't fear you, they approach you. They talk to you, and share things with you.

That's a very good thing, because you can engage in conversation with your team without having to remind them the whole time 'who's in charge.' You don't have to put your feet on the desk and lean back in the confident 'one of us can't get fired here' pose. You don't have to interrupt them because you *obviously* know what's best.

You don't need to talk *at* them—you can talk *with* them. And the more they talk with you, the more you'll see what they're good at. You'll figure out the best things they can offer the team and the company, and then you can shape their role to play to those strengths.

This will make your team succeed, and succeed fast.

And now you're thinking, *"How did I create an environment of competition? I need victors! They need spoils! May the best man-person win and all that!"*

It's okay. You don't need that old-boys-club attitude. Pitting people against each other when they are supposed to be working together just means they *don't* work together.

Instead, give your people something to be proud of. Something to own. Hand them a piece of the business to run that allows their strengths to shine.

When everyone gets to oversee something they're good at, and to share their stories with each other, your team will again succeed, and succeed fast.

Listen: no matter what you thought when you started, you don't have to 'lead like a man.'

You don't have to lead like the male bosses you see on television, in movies, in the news, in your office, in your friends' offices—the men who get raises, who get praised, who get promoted.

Instead, you can lead like *you*, and you'll still get the raises, the praise, the promotions.

So Kerri, it's okay to admit when managing people is hard. Everyone thinks so even if they don't say it.

It's okay if you cry in the bathroom when you need to. You won't be setting women back a hundred years.

It's okay to be called 'soft' when you don't turn everything into a confrontation. Be proud of your patience. You'll miss it on the days you can't find it.

And, after years of leading like you—looking after the team and the team's success—it's okay to walk away from it all if you want to do something else that will make you happier. You've earned it.

You've earned it all, and don't let anyone make you think otherwise.

LOVE,

Kerri

~

KERRI SHANNON STARTED WORKING AT MONEY MAP Press, a division of Agora, in February 2010 as an Associate Editor. She eventually developed and ran their first-ever editorial SEO initiative to generate record-high visitors for their flagship website, Moneymorning.com. She became Money Morning's first Editorial Director when the web and e-letter teams merged in 2015, and two years later was promoted to Money Morning Publisher. During her time at Money Map and previous jobs, she has been fortunate to have wonderful female and male leadership role models. She's also blessed with an incredible family who has taught her the value of hard work and respect for others—and are just fantastic people all around. When she's not at the office you can find her onstage performing improv comedy. You can find her comedic writing at Kerrishannon.com.

2

ANNIE HYMAN-PRATT

⁓

When you started listening, everything started to slowly change for the better.

DEAR ANNIE,

You are only in your twenties when your dad retires from The Coffee Bean and Tea Leaf. His health has been declining, and your degree in economics and successful finance career makes you a natural fit to take over the family business.

And you *are* a good fit. When you start, there were seven stores. And when you sell the company seven years later, there will be seventy. Sure, the 90s are a great time to be in the coffee industry, but your incredible work ethic and focus helps you scale at a rate that very few other companies can manage.

But that work ethic—and the belief that everyone else should be working just like you—will nearly cripple the entire business.

You will think you really know your stuff. Having grown up in the business, studied economics and worked in big finance, you will think you know more than everybody else there, that there is nothing left you need to learn.

So you really won't listen to your people. You will be a terrible micromanager, highly controlling and critical, and you really won't want to hear what anybody else has to say.

And because of that, your people will stop telling you things.

Soon you will be spending most of your time plugging gaps and scrambling to find short term fixes for the problems that keep blindsiding you. The business will lose a sickening amount of money as new stores miss their opening dates and key people start leaving.

But you still won't listen. You will push yourself to the edge of burnout, working longer and longer hours, and you will blame everybody else.

You will think that your employees just don't care as much as you do—that they aren't committed enough, don't work hard enough, and that if they would just do as you said, all these problems would go away.

You will decide that the only option is to lead by example, and so you will go into those stores and you will make coffee. You won't have a clue what you were doing, but if you don't do it the right way, they never will, right? You have to show them how hard you are willing to work, and that you don't expect anything of them that you wouldn't do yourself.

After one of these really long days playing 'boss barista', you will go back to the office, exhausted, to meet with your CFO. She has been trying to tell you that the regional managers are stretched too thin, but you just won't listen.

Don't they know how hard *you* are working? How much responsibility *you* have? That you have *already* told them the best way to fix their problems?

Eventually, your CFO will give up. She will storm out of the office, muttering something as she leaves—just loud enough for you to hear it—that will change your life forever.

"You're just a bitch in an ivory tower."

In hindsight, had you not been so shocked that you literally could not speak, you would have fired her on the spot. Luckily, you *were* that shocked, and all you could do was to sit there, slowly peeling your jaw off your ivory floor.

Soon afterwards, three of your best people came into your office and quit... and you panicked.

You finally realized that you had to listen.

You found a coach, and slowly began to see how your behaviour had been impacting everyone in the business. No matter how many systems you had in place, how much team building you tried, or how many leadership books you read, nothing would help you achieve the growth you wanted if you didn't listen to the people you were leading.

You realized that by going into stores to make coffee, you were signalling to them you didn't want them to step up, that you would rather do their work for them than leave it in their hands. When you refused to listen to their explanations of their problems, or refused to listen to their ideas, you were communicating that you didn't trust them or respect their experience.

So when you finally stopped blaming everybody, when you started listening, and gave them the space and support they actually needed, everything started to slowly change for the better.

You let go of the belief that you 'just weren't good with people', and stopped micromanaging everything. You learned to ask questions, so you could understand the experience and insights of the people who worked for you. You changed how you responded under stress, so that the team felt safe enough to tell you what was really going on, and you started involving them in creating solutions to our most pressing problems.

This period was one of the most painful and trying times of your life. It was worse than the migraines and anxiety you had as a teenager. It was worse than the sensitivity and self-consciousness that plagued you as a young adult.

It was so painful because you had to face up to the hard truth: it was all on you.

You had been blaming everyone else for your problems, and expecting your team to make up for your lack of true leadership. You had let your ego run wild over everyone else, and you had refused help at every turn.

But through all this suffering, you learned to understand and relate deeply to the pain and suffering of others. And fortunately, as time goes on, you'll learn to appreciate how we *all* suffer, and this discovery will lead to the biggest source of strength in your life: compassion.

Annie, the compassion you will learn to hold for yourself and others will become your "magic wand" later in life. It will allow you to heal deep hurts and turn pain into love. When you share your own experiences and struggles, not only will others appreciate your vulnerability and feel more connected to you, but it will free them to share their own struggles. Then you will be able to support each other naturally and openly.

And in that process of giving and receiving support, you'll experience the loving connection you crave, and which is surely one of the best parts of being human.

And always remember, no matter what happens, that I love you. Annie.

ANNIE HYMAN PRATT, KNOWN AS THE "TEAM Whisperer", develops Leaders and Teams that drive rapid growth and sustainable results—so Entrepreneurs can work on the strategic and visionary aspects of their business, while having the time, freedom, and impact they desire.

Annie more than 10x'd her family business—The Coffee

Bean and Tea Leaf—from a small local company to an International Brand of over seventy locations in seven years—then led the company through a highly successful sale.

Annie spent the next two decades as a Top-Tier Business Consultant specializing in "Rapid Growth and Change", guiding companies in many different industries through virtually every challenge and growth stage imaginable.

No other leadership or team development consultant comes close to Annie's level and scope of experience that's also integrated with a proven program. Her track record of success stems from her unique approach to business strategy, structure, systems, and the "missing link" of BEHAVIOR that brings it all together.

Whatever challenges you may be facing in your business, Annie has likely already seen it—and solved it. Some of Annie's current clients include fast-growing, high-level entrepreneurs like: Jeff Walker, Lisa Sasevich, Justin Livingston, Ryan Levesque, Christian Mickelsen and Reid Tracy.

❧ 3 ❧

MARY PIERCE BROSMER

~

In the middle of the journey of our life I found myself within a dark woods where the straight way was lost. — Dante Alighieri, *Inferno*

DEAR MARY-IN-THE-FIRST-GRADE WITH CROOKED BANGS, crooked bowtie, and winsome smile,

You are good at school (the "straight way" for a girl of your era and class), so much so that Sister Mary Aloysius seats you in the middle of the row where first grade borders second, so you can be a secret second grader.

You are fortunate and you know it. You are aware, early and always, of what has been given to you—education as the one thing that they can never take away from you, as your parents put it—and that this was a gift your parents had been prevented from receiving.

And yet, for all your education, you are already absorbing the story of silenced women. Of course, you will not be ready to write it until 1983, when your mother dies and your husband walks out of what you had believed to be your first safe home.

After your mother's death, you will decide to pick up your pen and begin to live, by writing a different story. Reading others' words, and teaching them is your straight way within the dark woods of a culture made by men, for men.

Here's a small poem you will write about that:

MUSE
    Isabel Rose Caliendo Pierce
      (May 12, 1918–April 11, 1983)

> *The lurch of your leaving pushed*
> *poetry from me, working class girl*
> *taught only poems by my betters,*
> *words by girls from storied families*
> *with names like Dickinson, Lowell*
> *which education was, to me, the same*
> *as being taught that girls from unstoried*
> *families, as if there were such a thing,*
> *could not write their own, only read*
> *(or teach) others' poems.*

> *Mother, I feel you listening in the ether,*
> *to this story I repeat in both poetry and prose:*

> *I, Mary Lucille,*
> *learned most of what I know to do*
> *for the sake of love, from you,*
> *Isabel Rose.*

At that moment, in the middle of the journey of your life,

you will have a series of dreams, and write a series of poems that will change everything for you—and for many other women and girls.

These dreams will, in time, lead you to create Women Writing for (a) Change—a community led by women, for women, to nurture and celebrate the individual voice. These dreams will lead you to facilitate supportive writing circles and to encourage women to craft more conscious lives through the art of writing and the practices of community.

But when you have your first dream, you will still be hewing to the straight way of traditional schools, and you're already wondering why it all makes you feel so tired.

> *I carry my briefcase wearily home to my mother's kitchen. I walk into a circle of her friends, their names a litany of such sweetness, I awaken to tears: Marge, Dot, Esther, Billie, Elsie, and Betty. Mama Isabel, beaming, says, "sit down, Mary, you look tired. Put your briefcase down."*

After you finish your M.A. in Literature, you will be hired to teach Studies in Women's Literature at Xavier University, and you will anticipate a longed-for opportunity to bring women's words to the table, without having to justify "teaching all those women."

It is not to be. The question simply mutates: *Why are you teaching all these feminists? Why are you teaching so many lesbians?*

Despite your most skillful facilitation, despite the strenuous efforts to speak and be heard on the part of "non-traditional" (female) students, the semester becomes an exhausting battle of the sexes.

You will struggle to hear the women, they to hear you, and all of us to hear the women writers we had assembled to hear, above the din of indignant male voices demanding explanation, justification.

You will laugh ruefully about how women talk in stolen

moments, in the hallway during breaks, going to and from class, in the "women's room."

Marcella Allison, recently graduated from the University of Chicago with an English degree (and who will cross over with you to the land of WWfaC) writes: *"Why do we always have to teach the boys?"*

It is against this backdrop you have your second dream:

> *I begin to take roll in Women's Lit class and realize all the*
> *men—half the class—are absent!*
> *I keep wondering why they signed up for a course in women's literature they're prepared to hate!*
> *I curse this latest "tactic" on their part.*
> *I am worried about the strength of my words at the last class,*
> *did I come on too strong?*
>
> *The scene metamorphoses and now we are all women seated around a beautiful mahogany table with lace cloth.*
> *We are in a Victorian-era house, and we begin to talk immediately and passionately about the literature at hand.*
> *The lights blink and go out. The atmosphere grows ominous.*
> *We have to abandon our studies to focus on the threat to our environment.*

AND THE THIRD DREAM:

*I am teaching women only; we are sitting around a table
writing plays, and they keep coming up with plays about
sexual abuse. I am bewildered, and afraid of what will
happen to us if we keep writing about such things.
I have no impulse to contain or control, but much fear.*

*In the next part of the dream
I am hiding in an old Victorian house from people
who are trying to kill me because of the teaching
I am daring to do.*

AFTER RECORDING THIS DREAM, YOU WRITE IN YOUR JOURNAL
the draft of what became the first Women Writing for (a)
Change brochure, describing the values and vision of a school
where women can find their voices, speak their truths and tell
their stories in a world in which they were often silenced. You
will always call it a school, and yourself a teacher.

When you leave Xavier to establish Women Writing for (a)
Change in 1991, you will feel yourself to be in exile. But unlike
Dante, you were not exiled; you *chose* exile. It was the only space
in which you could learn what you came to learn, and teach what
you came to teach.

And unlike Dante, who spent his life longing to return to the
center of power he occupied in Florence, you will never—for one
moment for the rest of your life—want to return to what was,
because there is no center of power you will ever experience that
is transparent about where power comes from and how it is used.

Mary, it will take a long trek through the dark woods of
patriarchy to come to the clear realization that any organization
—even those with missions of rescuing and protecting victims of
runaway patriarchy—*will reproduce patriarchy,* as long as it runs on
the engines and fuel of the masculine-only.

So let me warn you, lovingly, that the most difficult challenge
you will face—and the most valuable gift you will contribute—

will come about when you decide to bring the depth of feminine practices into these systems which rely solely, and destructively, on the masculine.

You name it "Caring for the Container" at Women Writing for (a) Change, and it is at the core of the the powerful, transformative communities you will create.

When you were a high school teacher, you opened every class with a student reading the "class log." She or he had the responsibility (and opportunity) to describe in both practical and personal terms the previous day's class. Later, you will spend *decades* trying to get schools, start-ups, established businesses, and troubled and traumatized groups to incorporate a variation of this process, where the group uses writing circle practices to create a safe and nurturing space for each person to share their writing and the truths of their lives.

You will name it an "Organizational Operating System," and, in the wake of increased violence, an "Empathy Operating System." You are so passionate about it that you refer to it in a 2010 TEDx Talk as "The Holy Grail of Organizational Wholeness."

You know that human beings know ourselves and create ourselves through language. However, we are more guarded and political when we "just talk." A group that writes regularly together can learn that multiple truths and points of view are valuable as opposed to a group reduced to group-think.

Where there are more truths, there are fewer rumors. While conversation and debate privilege those with the most power in a group, the Organizational Operating System enfranchises the entire system.

Creating health in dysfunctional systems is a process, not a commodity or "fix." Moving into a new paradigm is risky, and care should be taken to go slowly and with compassion, but not to give in to resistance and the many forms it takes by giving up.

Remember that everyone is afraid and everyone is vulnerable; remember, too, that fear and vulnerability can be transformed to courage and compassion when there is a safe container to facilitate that transformation. You have taught thousands of women—and men too —to embrace this empathic operating system, to care for the container, and to hold the space that allows transformational change to occur.

So finding OurSelf nearing the end of this journey, young Mary, I hold your slight body against mine matured, in an embrace of gratitude for all the steps, even (especially) the ones that felt like missteps, falls, failings.

We made space, as we were able, for OurSelf and others to inscribe:

> *a newer testament, a fragile scripture*
> *refusing savior or sainthood, icon,*
> *cathedral, pyramid, haj or hashtag*
> *refusing rising again, for the miracle*
> *of opening to love*
> *again and again and again.*

(FROM "FRAGILITY, EASTER EVE, 2018", MPB)

ALL MY LOVE,
  Mary.

∽

MARY PIERCE BROSMER IS A WRITER, TRANSFORMATIVE educator and systems thinker who brings the art of writing and the practices of community to the work of organizational well-being and social healing in business, political, medical and educational settings.

Mary is a published poet and author of *Women Writing for (a)*

Change: A Guide for Creative Transformation (Notre Dame: Sorin Press, 2009). Mary is a TEDx speaker, presenting "Found: the Holy Grail of Organizational Wholeness" at TEDxCincy, October, 2010. She can be reached at: mpierce@womenwriting.org

❀ 4 ❀

TEPSII THENDO LUFUNO TSHIKORORO

~

Tomorrow. It starts tomorrow. Tomorrow I am living differently than I am living today.

TEPSII,

On January 19th, you were sitting up in bed. Your third baby was sleeping next to you, hot and making you all sweaty. It was like all the other nights you had lain awake thinking about what a disappointment you were.

You're just a breeder. You don't have the degrees your family wanted for you. You're flakey and can't make anything work.

But that night, listening to your baby breathing, you thought about going back to work the next day and hated the idea. You wondered what it would be like for your kids to spend their lives with somebody else caring for them. You wondered what it would be like for yourself, to spend your life facing the slow erosion of your self-respect and tenacious attitude.

In that moment you decided that you were no longer going to accept the status quo for your life. You decided that tomorrow was the day that everything would change.

It did. And you were scared to death.

There was all the risk that every freelancer or entrepreneur takes on, but the scariest thing was that you couldn't see anyone like you doing what you wanted to do. There were no moms, and no prominent people of color in the space. Everyone seemed to be blonde, always very made up and laughing over their location-independent laptops on a beach somewhere. You were afraid you wouldn't be accepted for who you were in this new space

Well, let me tell you something Tepsii. You didn't see those faces when you got started, but you have become that face for other people. Not seeing other people that look like you doesn't mean there's not space for you — it means that you get to create that space and become that role model for yourself, and for others.

Growing up in South Africa during apartheid, you know how powerful it can be when people get rooted in a purpose bigger than themselves, and then use their voices and their self-expression to communicate that purpose.

And you know the sacrifices people made to move that purpose forward, and to get you where you are today. People died. People went to prison, lost all their possessions, were excommunicated from their communities—your family and their friends suffered, a lot, to create change in the world.

So you choose to show up, and to use the voice you've cultivated to speak on behalf of those who don't yet have their own voices. Writing has always given you the ability to express yourself and allowed you to enter into spaces you might not have been welcome otherwise. It has made you into a revolutionary, a renegade, someone who doesn't accept the status quo, and with it you start to champion diversity in your industry.

Your ability to create change and drives you on. Democracy is not easy, and it requires all of us to speak up. As a copywriter and someone who has the ability of self expression, you get to fight in a very different way. You show up to the front lines to show people that they get to choose what to do with their own lives, no matter where they are starting from, and no matter if they can't see faces like their own doing it yet.

People start reaching out to you to say that you've given them the courage to start their own businesses. Others tell you that you helped them step up and make the scary decisions in their own lives. One woman emulated your launch process, made $10,000 and was able to walk away from an abusive marriage as a result. You *are* the change you want to see in the world.

So when you're afraid, when you're feeling small, when you think you're just a breeder who will never amount to anything, show up anyway.

Acknowledge your self-doubt and fear, but check them. You will not always go to bed disappointed. One day you will step into your greatness, you will bring healing to people all around the world, you will take up the space you deserve, and you will get to show up powerfully and passionately every day.

Tepsii.

I'M TEPSII THENDO LUFUNO TSHIKORORO, AND AS a Business Coach and Copywriter, I offer strategy, consultation, and copywriting to help entrepreneurs ready to make serious moola online create the oh-so-coveted freedom lifestyle they've always dreamt of.

I've been a sought after professional writer in the corporate space for twelve years using my bachelor's of science from a top university in New England to write scientific, engineering, aviation, and other technical documentation (SNOOZEFEST)!

For many years, I've been dying to merge my creative side

with my work. So, after I had my third (and freaking-cute and freaking-final) baby girl I decided to get serious about creating a life of my own design. For me, this meant ditching the boring nine-to-five where I was busy making someone else's dreams come true.

Now, I've found my sweet spot; I get to help entrepreneurs by creating businesses they truly love. As a working mom of three, my family is my life! Life revolves around my family and they fuel my entrepreneurial drive. They're my reason for everything (you're more than likely to see them occasionally pop in while we're working!)

Within my first two months in biz I made a cool $25,000, left my corporate job and moved back home (after twenty-something years away) to my dream location, South Africa.

My life hasn't always been steady on cruise control, though. I lost my mom in a car accident when I was fourteen; was homeless, survived domestic abuse at the hands of my first husband; and, got divorced all before I was twenty-two. But you won't catch me wallowing over all that because I'm still standing and still smiling. I've been able to move through and heal from those events because they don't define me! Who wants a pity-party when they can throw a rockstar bash?

I believe in taking responsibility for my healing, my mindset, and my intentions. My dynamic life experiences combined with my extensive professional training give me an intuitive ability to zoom in on your strengths and help you bring your ideal customer, products, and passion to life.

5

SARAH HINER

~

Don't be afraid to do things differently, to create a new legacy.

DEAR SARAH—

So, you want to be President of Bottom Line. There is an old saying you might want to keep in mind: be careful what you wish for, because you just might get it.

It's been nearly five years now since you got your wish. Depending on how you measure it, you have either been an enormous success, or an enormous failure.

The company has been profitable every year since you became President, you created a fresh brand strategy and direction for the company, and most importantly, we are still in business when many of our competitors are barely hanging on, or have been put up for sale. But we haven't nailed the digital transformation yet, in spite of multiple attempts, and we are not out of the woods.

However you look at it, there are a whole lot of lessons you need to be prepared for.

The biggest challenge is that you are heading into a world where nothing is the same as it used to be. There is no one to guide you in how to get there, wherever 'there' is, and so you're going to have to pull on your big-girl pants and get ready for some big things to come your way.

First, let go of legacy. Your dad, who started this company, was a visionary when developing Bottom Line's flagship publications, and a genius at editorial and marketing copy. But everything he did was in the formula of the day, and that day is gone.

Don't be afraid to do things differently, to create a new legacy. If you don't, you will fail. Dad's legacy and achievements are locked safely in time, and your job now is to evolve the business and brand for the present and the future.

Ask yourself what brand equity needs to be maintained, what old assumptions and models need to be released, what Bottom Line's modern customers need, and how your team can fulfill those needs in a unique way. Find the intersection of the answers to these questions, point your finger in that direction and lead the way.

Understand that you may eventually be running two businesses in one. You've seen old bridges left in place while new ones are constructed around them to meet the world's changing needs, and you are doing the same thing here: building a whole new business that will surround and eventually replace the old one.

The traditional print business, whose aging audience is loyal to our brand and content formats, will at some point have to give way to the online side of the business, which leverages our best content to get our brand in front of a new generation of customers. But your challenge will be getting the new customers to pay like the old ones did, when they have been trained that content online should be free, and so you will have to walk a fine line between the two models as your team tries to work it out.

It's for this reason that *"because we've always done it like that"* simply won't fly anymore.

Everything must be up for review, no matter how big or small. There will be people who want to maintain the status quo, and you must inspire them past their resistance. Don't accept any excuses—if we don't evolve, we will become the next buggy whip. As President, you will revamp processes in every part of the company, and the resulting savings and increased efficiency are so exciting to see.

But not everyone can get on board with change. Remember that people will come and go, and while there is nothing more painful for a leader than to let people go, the new world we're in requires new people with new skills. Think of it like playing for the Super Bowl—sometimes good players get traded to other teams, and you must make those trades if the player doesn't fit the game plan you are laying out.

That said, it's going to be especially tricky hiring the new generation of digital experts. The "millennials" are super smart, but they need a lot of training on standard business procedure, and most importantly, need to understand our brand values. The immediacy of everything online means that they tend to think in the short-term, transactionally, rather than with the long-term, relational perspective that is critical for brands to succeed. Never forget that you are rebuilding a powerful brand from the ground up, and this long-term focus is critical.

The culture will be incredibly difficult to change. It's important to retain the warm, informal, familial feel of the company, but it's time for the team to build up the entrepreneurial, all-hands-on-deck mentality again that Dad expected in the early days. Every person on the team needs to be signed onto the mission of relaunching this brand, and the tipping point of changing the culture will require far more than the infusion of 'fresh blood.' Besides bringing in players from the brave new world, you will have to constantly reinforce the vision and culture of the company, personally leading through meetings, individual interactions, and corporate communications, relying on your unwavering belief in the new direction you have set.

Remember, always, that you are in uncharted territory. There's no right answer here, so there are no mistakes—only attempts to find out what works. When something doesn't work, pivot and let it go. Pivoting is the name of the game in this new economy. Keep in mind that your competitors are wading their way through the same quagmire.

Last but not least, be kind to yourself. This stuff is hard. Really hard. And it's going to be lonely, sitting in that big green chair in your office. Cut yourself some slack—you might feel lonely, but you're not alone. Your team is with you, and they are evolving to meet these new challenges.

With love and admiration,

Your future self.

SARAH HINER IS PRESIDENT AND CEO OF BOTTOM LINE Inc., a multi-media provider of expert-sourced advice for your health, money and home, including books and consumer newsletters Bottom Line Health and Bottom Line Personal and bottomlineinc.com.

Sarah, a lecturer and writer, has a passion for people having the tools and knowledge they need to be in control of their own lives as it pertains, in particular, to women's health, the challenges of the healthcare system, common-sense financial advice and family life. She appears often on national radio, and hosts a podcast, The Bottom Line Advocator, talking about her belief that people have more control over all areas of their lives than they realize, and how Bottom Line's expert advice helps them gain that power.

Sarah spent her early career at Grey Advertising on large consumer packaged goods accounts and at several boutique ad agencies in New York and Colorado. She has also owned her own marketing consultancy and hosted a weekly radio show, Bottom Line On Your Health.

When she's not working, Sarah enjoys skiing and hiking with her husband, two daughters and dog, in the mountains of Colorado.

❧ 6 ❧

JENNY THOMPSON

~

When things are uncertain, you know how
to step into the breach.

JENNY,

You were ten years old when you learned to lead. Your
parents divorced, your mother had a breakdown, and in the
months that followed you discovered that nobody was in charge
in your home anymore.

You learned to get by, to get yourself to school on time and to
cover for your rebellious older sister. Yes, you lived in a good
neighborhood, there was food in the fridge and you wanted for
very little, but those years shaped you. They made you who you
are and prepared you to become the leader you are today.

Five lessons emerged from the microcosm of your early
life, and to this day, they have never let you down.

LESSON ONE: SOMEONE HAS TO BE IN CHARGE.

It doesn't have to be you. You are not a control freak; you are a 'someone has to be in control' freak. Your time at Agora Publishing gave you an unshakeable confidence in your leadership, problem-solving and decision-making abilities, and when things are uncertain, you know how to step into the breach. If someone else is leading, you will happily let them lead. But if no one is steering the ship, you will step up and find a solution very quickly.

That is not to say you're a perfect leader—you make mistakes every day. You say things you shouldn't, and sometimes your ideas don't stand up to testing. But leadership is about steering that ship whether the seas are calm or stormy or full of sharks, and you have built the fundamental skills throughout your life to do that wherever you find yourself.

LESSON TWO: HEAR WHAT PEOPLE SAY ABOUT YOU.

During college, you got a job as a bailiff. You had been looking for a summer job in administration. But the woman who interviewed you really liked your energy and couldn't see you pushing papers all day. You took the next year off college because you were having so much fun running those courtrooms (though the sheriff never did let you hold his gun).

Your dad used to say that when ten people tell you you're drunk, lie down. When people tell you you're great or smart or funny or energetic, notice that you are hearing this thing repeatedly and *embrace it*.

Many people throughout your life will tell you that you have great energy—you walk into a room and can take over it very quickly. Instead of letting that make you feel insecure or shrinking away from it, build your brand and career and strength around it. So many women apologize for the characteristics that make them who they are, when they could make that the thing about themselves that is remarkable, not just noticeable.

And understand that if enough people tell you something about yourself, whether it's positive or negative, it's true. If it's a positive thing then run with it, but if it's negative then you have to acknowledge that it's a strong, noticeable part of who you are, and you have to decide how you're going to deal with that. Embrace that they're right, even if you're not going to embrace the quality they are commenting on.

LESSON THREE: YOUR WORK IS A RELATIONSHIP.

You graduated from the University of Maryland and while you really wanted to go up to New York City to work on Madison Avenue and be an advertising mogul, you met your ex-husband and stayed in Maryland. You fell into work in non-profit communications. They were not non-profits you felt good about working for, and the work was not challenging.

It wasn't until you took a role as a direct marketing manager with The Oxford Club at Agora that you realized how fulfilling work could be.

It was a place where people embraced risk and ideas and strength of ideas, and disagreement. You could debate about why you would do something and everything would be tested, so if people had varying ideas, you could test them and see which one was right.

Moving to Agora showed you just how amazing work could be on a day to day basis. You saw then that a job that drains your energy, drains your drive and makes you feel bad is just like a romantic relationship you have to leave or you'll never find the thing that's right for you.

Think about doing work you love in the same way you would use a dating app—only swipe right on the candidates that really appeal to you and are a fit for how you want to grow in your life.

LESSON FOUR: FIRE FAST; BE THE PERSON DURING THAT YOU WANT TO BE AFTER.

Your father, wise man that he was, once told you that if you are going to fire somebody, fire them right away. When you let people linger, it becomes very destructive. You can overpay them in severance and give them whatever you need to, but once you decide to fire somebody, act quickly.

That's a very hard thing for women to do. We always want to give people another chance. We feel that we didn't give them enough support, that we failed them in some way (and sometimes we did).

But one of your favorite philosophies in business and relationships is that it doesn't matter if it's your fault or not—it doesn't work. Mentos and Diet Coke don't sit there trying to figure out why they don't get along. You just can't put them together; it doesn't matter why.

And at the end of any relationship—when you're firing someone, quitting a company or leaving a marriage—where there is any potential for drama, be the person during it that you want to be after it.

Be the kindest, calmest, most giving person you can be in that moment. Be more generous with severance and notice and alimony than you think you should be. Be the person you want to be in every circumstance, because if you let anger and bitterness get to you, it will change who you are, right down to your emotional DNA.

LESSON FIVE: ALWAYS HAVE FUCK-YOU MONEY.

You've always said that you're willing to die on your own sword, but not on someone else's. And if you don't have money, you don't have a sword.

Your mother was not prepared for her divorce. She was not financially independent at all—she was a stay at home mom, she had been an English lit major in college, had never had a job and didn't see it was coming. You don't remember hearing your parents ever yell at each other until the morning your father said he was leaving.

She was painfully unprepared and in that moment you decided that you would never let that happen to you, that you would never let someone blindside you so much that everything gets taken away in a moment.

And ironically enough, it was your father, again, who showed you how. He told you that you should always have fuck-you money—enough money that you can walk away from any situation without hesitation.

Financial independence doesn't mean wealth—it means that you can live within your means and you have access to your own money. You know what your lifestyle costs, and you are not reliant on a partner or a credit card to maintain that lifestyle.

All the women in the #MeToo movement—every one of them—would have had the option to tell those men to go fuck themselves, and leave, if they had been financially independent. That doesn't mean their experiences wouldn't negatively impact them, but money gives you freedom to choose what you are exposed to.

Even though you came from a good background, after college you were poor to a degree that terrified you. For months you didn't know if you would make your rent, and you and your husband had to play around with when you paid the bills just to make each dollar stretch far enough. But you still invested in your 401K with every paycheck, and put money in your savings with every paycheck. You might have lived on ramen noodles and sachets of Kool Aid for months, and cried for two hours after spending $50 on shoes when you finally got a job, but you always knew that financial independence was the most important thing you could build for yourself.

And when you got divorced, you could afford to walk away, and be the generous person you wanted to be. When you left

Agora, you could afford to take a gamble on starting a tech company, and it was all because you had prioritized your financial independence from day one.

So keep it up. You're in a whole new world now, with this tech business, surrounded by a different breed of marketers and developers, but you know you could run any business. This too is exciting, fulfilling work, so trust your abilities, trust your instincts, and trust your ability to lead.

Jenny.

IN 1996, JENNY THOMPSON MADE ONE OF THE MOST important decisions of her life: To leave her Dilbertian job and answer an ad in the *Baltimore Sun* for a marketing manager. Soon after, she joined the team at Agora Inc. She began her career with the company at The Oxford Club. In her first year there, she tripled profits. On the heels of that success, the owners asked her to take over the fledging health business. After just 10 months there, she increased the bottom line 500%. In that role, Jenny introduced over a dozen additional paid and free newsletters, launched 3 supplement lines, and acquired a skincare company. At its peak, NewMarket Health marketed 18 paid and free newsletters, more than 70 dietary supplements, and 8 skincare products to more than 1.2 million customers and prospects around the world.

In 2016, with the business projected to hit $70 million, Jenny made the decision to let the next generation take over and go out on her own. Using her "blink" style marketing and business management strategy, she took off running to help create magic in growing businesses. She is now the founder of SafetyPIN Technologies, the best way to know someone you met online is safe to meet offline. And assure them that you are, too.

EPILOGUE

I HOPE THE LESSONS IN THESE PAGES HAVE ENCOURAGED YOU, challenged you, and inspired you. I hope you have found yourself in these stories. I hope you have discovered that you are *not* alone. And most of all, I hope you have felt what it's like to have dozens of female mentors cheering you on and leading the way.

The Not-So-Secret Order of the Titanides is about mentorship by community. It is about collective mentoring by women, for women. Our community is founded on the belief that we all have something to share about our journey that can help another woman. You do not need to know everything, you just need to know a little bit more than the woman coming behind you. You just need to share that next step with her, to show her the way.

You see, I believe that those of us who have succeeded in the testosterone-driven business world have a duty to stand up and hold the door open for the next woman in line. I believe that once we have achieved a certain level of success, we have a responsibility to pay it forward and advocate for other women.

I'm a firm believer that the only way to change the world is to start in your own backyard. I'm starting by making it my mission to encourage, support, and empower more women... to become leaders, to speak, to mentor, to teach.

Because the fact is, it's very hard to find female mentors at the highest levels of almost any industry. That's why I founded the Titanides and that's why I've asked these extraordinary women to share their truth with you. Because the only way we will have more female mentors is for all of us to step up to the plate and become mentors ourselves. This is how we all move forward together.

If you like what you've read here, if you want to benefit from the wisdom and generosity of this community of women, if you're looking for experienced mentors to show you the way, then I hope you'll join us at Titanides.com.

And if you're a seasoned marketer, entrepreneur or copywriter, then I hope you'll join us and share your wisdom and knowledge with other women. Please help us to pay-it-forward and empower the next generation of women in business.

MARCELLA ALLISON
    Founder of The Not-So-Secret Order of the Titanides
    Cincinnati, 2019.

WANT MORE OF THE TITANIDES?

The letters in this book were inspired by a short journaling exercise called Fearless Fast Writes. Fearless Fast Writes can spark new ideas or projects, boost productivity, and help you overcome creative blocks in your writing and business. Best of all, the exercise takes just five minutes to complete, and you do not have to be a writer to participate.

This shared journaling practice was first developed by fellow Titanide, Mary Pierce Brosmer for her school, Women Writing For (A) Change. Since then it's been adapted by the Titanides as a powerful tool for creating community, co-mentoring, and connection between women.

If you would like to see what it's like to tap into your creativity in a safe, supportive, circle of strong women, then please join us free of charge for the next Titanides Fast Write. Simply go to *www.titanides.com/book* to register.

Here's just a sample of what you can expect from a Fearless Fast Write:

"What a deep experience, to spend such a short amount of time and get to know you all (and myself) so much better... it's like a light in the middle of my otherwise everyday day! Thanks, all!"
  - Joyce Hollman

"All I could keep thinking was, 'I am so honored to be in the midst of such fine, brave women.' Thank you."
  - Mary Rose Maguire

"Fun, warm, raw, validating, joyful! Big hugs to all!"
  - Shelley Ware

Plus, when you go to *www.titanides.com/book* you'll also discover exclusive bonus material, from our collected authors.

You'll find insider secrets, exclusive tools, and pro tips by some of the best women in marketing, copywriting, and entrepreneurship. We want you to thrive in all areas of your personal and professional life. There's no charge. This is our way of paying it forward to others.

And if you would like to join the conversation in the vibrant, supportive community of women that is the Titanides, go to: https://www.facebook.com/groups/Titanides/

Onward!

ACKNOWLEDGMENTS

I have a confession to make: I'm so terrified of leaving someone out or committing an egregious error that I almost left off the acknowledgements altogether. So if I've accidentally left you out, please know that I do love you but I'm older now and my memory isn't what it used to be. Forgive me.

To all the women who participated in this project and were willing to share their stories and their journeys with the world so that other women and men might benefit from their wisdom, thank you.

To Laura Gale who trusted me enough to take this crazy two-year journey with me. You held our hearts in your hands and you helped to show us our truth. Without you there would be no book. Thank you.

To Jen Adams, my equity partner in the Titanides, who is always there at 2 a.m. to balance the books, brainstorm ideas, fill the coffers, vent or celebrate as the occasion warrants. You're a breast-feeding multi-tasking resource-slinging knight in shining armor.

To my sister, Jennifer Wells, who helped midwife the first edition of the book and organized the entire project from the beginning. This book is as much your baby as mine.

To the entire Titanides team, past and present, for co-creating this book and this community and paying it forward to so many women in so many ways. Karina Bone, Pauline Longdon, Chris Allsop, Joyce Hollman, Bernie Boyd, and Mary Gruen. Thank you.

To Denise Ford, Katie Yeakle, Rebecca Matter, and all the women at American Writers and Artists, Inc. who believed and supported the Titanides from the very beginning. Thank you for your faith in us.

To Mary Pierce Brosmer, the founder of Women Writing for (a) Change, who taught me how to create community, how to care for the container, and how to use the power of words to change the world for the better.

To Lois Mentrup, Shannon Housley, Belinda Brewster and all the women who have worked with me at Copy Harvest, thank you for always having my back.

To Monica Day, coach, instigator, and ass-kicker extraordinaire, who encouraged me to start my own freelance copywriting firm more than a decade ago and showed me the way.

To Michele Wolk, Carmen Suarez, Cindy Butehorn, Chrissy Borchardt, Serena Savage, Ellyn Bader, and all the bad-ass women entrepreneurs, copychiefs, and project managers I've been lucky enough to work with over the years.

To all my intrepid mid-western prairie ancestors who taught me the meaning of true grit without which I would have given up a long time ago.

And to all the men who encourage and support the Titanides despite the fact that they have the wrong equipment to join...

To Tom Allison, my husband of twenty-eight years, for always loving me, encouraging me, and supporting me.

To Brian Kurtz, who gave me my first shot at writing for Boardroom Inc. when I was just starting out in the business and who continues to mentor me today. Thank you for inspiring me to start the Titanides.

To Parris Lampropoulos and David Deutsch who mentored me and encouraged me and shared all their best copywriting secrets with me.

To Henry Bingaman for sharing more crazy adventures than I can count, lending me some swagger, and teaching and chiefing with me.

To Kevin Rogers, 'the only rooster in the hen house', who shares my passion and vision for creating community.

To Mike Ward and the entire team at Money Map Press for giving me a place to shine and for opening the door for more female financial copywriters.

To Ben Settle, who likes to pretend to be an asshole and then secretly supports the Titanides with scholarships and mentoring. I've got your number.

To John Carlton who supported female copywriters and

entrepreneurs long before it was cool or hip. Thank you for carving a path for the rest of us rebels to follow.

And most of all, thank you to all the Titanides who make this community a safe, vital supportive place for female marketers, copywriters and entrepreneurs to grow and thrive.

Marcella.